THE REFERENCE SHELF   VOLUME 34 NUMBER 4

REPRESENTATIVE AMERICAN SPEECHES: 1961-1962

EDITED BY LESTER THONSSEN

Professor of Speech, The City College of New York

THE H. W. WILSON COMPANY

NEW YORK   1962

THE REFERENCE SHELF

The books in this series reprint articles, excerpts from books, and addresses on current issues, social trends, and other aspects of American life, and occasional surveys of foreign countries. There are six separately bound numbers in each volume, all of which are generally published in the same calendar year. One number is a collection of recent speeches on a variety of subjects; each of the remaining numbers is devoted to a single subject and gives background information and discussion from varying points of view, followed by a comprehensive bibliography.

Subscribers to the current volume receive the books as issued. The subscription rate is $10 ($12 foreign) for a volume of six numbers. The price of single numbers is $2.50 each.

Copyright © 1962
By The H. W. Wilson Company
Library of Congress Catalog Card No. (38-27962)

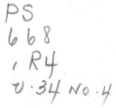

PS
668
.R4
v.34 No.4

PREFACE

With understandable frequency the major speeches of 1961-1962 sounded a familiar and frightening note: national security in a deepening world crisis. Rare indeed was the address which did not, in one way or another, link its theme with the threatened eclipse of freedom or the possibility of mass destruction of the human race. Speakers in and out of government underscored the wisdom of Aristotle's remark that a principal subject on which orators speak is war and peace.

Whether or not the leaders of all political persuasions got their messages through to the people was debatable. Astute news analysts believed that many Americans remained more concerned about the outcome of the home run contests and the daytime serials than about the grim prospect of thermonuclear war. Commenting on his trip through the country in late 1961, New York *Times* correspondent James Reston spoke of the mood of many Americans as a mixture of "fatalism and confidence." Many people, baffled by the talk about fantastic military weapons and space exploration, are convinced, Reston remarked, "that they are living in a world they cannot understand." Herman Kahn, onetime consultant to the Atomic Energy Commission and author of *On Thermonuclear War,* spoke similarly of the average American's fatalistic attitude. " 'If we're all going to be dead anyway,' the people argue, 'there's no use thinking about it.' "

Such remarks are relevant to any study of the effect of speechmaking on society. As one of the important media of communication, the spoken word can provide enlightenment, create readiness for action, and shape a national mood consistent with the necessities of the time. In fact, the words are of themselves, as Sidney Hyman, Washington political analyst, has said, "a mode of action." Through the use of words, the leader "hauls problems to the center of the political stage, sets forth the priorities for dealing with them, defines alternative solutions to the problems, and seeks to win the assent of his many constituencies to the particular solution he embraces." If in 1961 the public did not appreciate sufficiently the dimension of the world crisis, or take it seriously enough, what did the major speeches lack in substance or manner, or both? Why did they fail to convey a full sense of emergency which the gravity of the world's plight demanded?

These questions are thorny. But they strike at a disturbing paradox in the process of communication. On the one hand, leaders must educate by exposing the great issues and stirring the people to a realistic acknowledgment of danger; on the other, they must transmit a sense of urgency without inducing panic. All of this must be done, moreover, without divulging information which must be kept secret in the interests of national security.

Many of the recent talks on conditions at home and abroad were uncommonly good. And they were not devoid of fervor. Whether or not the highest officials delivered enough speeches to all of the people on both international and domestic issues, and at reasonable intervals, is problematical. The process of education always uses time and patience as its allies. Repetition and refrain are necessary ingredients. It is conceivable that we had too little rather than too much talk last year.

This edition, twenty-fifth in the series, reflects the continuing cooperation of speakers in giving permission to reprint their addresses. Public officers and private citizens alike have assisted me generously in providing copies of addresses which I was eager to examine. As in the past, colleagues and friends have alerted me to many speeches which might otherwise have escaped my notice. For special help I am indebted to John Jamieson and Ruth Ulman of The H. W. Wilson Company, Dorothea Thonssen, C. W. Reynolds, Margaret Robb of the University of Colorado, Ota Thomas Reynolds of Hunter College, Donald J. Gonzales of Colonial Williamsburg, and Thomas Nickerson and Shunzo Sakamaki of the University of Hawaii.

LESTER THONSSEN

New York City
July 1962

CONTENTS

A Closer Look at the Stars

SOLEMN WORDS ON THE FATEFUL CHALLENGE

THE BERLIN CRISIS [1]

JOHN F. KENNEDY [2]

Americans with good memory of what went on in the 1930's and early 1940's doubtless found in President Kennedy's radio-television address to the nation on July 25, 1961, a poignant reminder that this generation has never been far removed from crises. Thoughts went back to March 12, 1933, when, in his first fireside chat, President Franklin D. Roosevelt told what the banking emergency meant to the people; or to December 29, 1940, when, in his call for full response on national defense, he solemnly announced:

> The Nazi masters of Germany have made it clear that they intend not only to dominate all life and thought in their own country, but also to enslave the whole of Europe, and then to use the resources of Europe to dominate the rest of the world.

With no less gravity, President Kennedy announced his preliminary program to meet the Soviet challenge. Ever since his return from the meetings with President de Gaulle, Premier Khrushchev, and Prime Minister Macmillan in early June 1961, the President had devoted the greater share of his time to the foreign rather than the domestic scene. In the speech of June 6, delivered upon his return from the Vienna conference with Mr. Khrushchev, the President had reminded the nation that "a hard struggle must be our fate as Americans in this generation as the chief defenders of the cause of liberty."

By late July the Berlin crisis neared a climax. Mr. Khrushchev was insisting that the condition in West Berlin be "normalized" and that the solution be reached within six months. If no agreement were reached, the Soviet Union would, Mr. Khrushchev intimated, sign a separate peace treaty with East Germany. This would affect freedom of access to Berlin for the Western powers.

Speaking from his desk in the Oval Room of the White House, the President boldly declared America's resolve not to be driven out of Berlin, "either gradually or by force." To be ready "to resist with force, if force is used upon us," he specified the measures necessary for the

---

[1] Text furnished by Pierre Salinger, press secretary to the President, with permission for this reprint.

[2] For biographical note, see Appendix.

preservation of freedom and peace. They included increased military spending, additions to the authorized strength of the Army, and greater emphasis on civil defense.

While the tone of the address was serious, it was not belligerent. The New York *Times* called it a speech that was "at once solemn, determined and conciliatory." The President repeated this country's intention to listen to any proposals which sought genuine understanding. "To sum it all up: We seek peace—but we shall not surrender. That is the central meaning of this crisis—and the meaning of this Government's policy."

The reaction to the speech both in America and allied capitals was uniformly enthusiastic. The President had seemingly struck a fine balance between a proclamation of strength and a declaration of willingness to engage in responsible negotiation. "It is good," said the Prime Minister of Nigeria, that "the door is left open for discussion."

Seven weeks ago tonight I returned from Europe to report on my meeting with Premier Khrushchev and the others. His grim warnings about the future of the world, his aide-mémoire on Berlin, his subsequent speeches and threats which he and his agents have launched, and the increase in the Soviet military budget that he has announced, have all prompted a series of decisions by the Administration and a series of consultations with the members of the NATO organization. In Berlin, as you recall, he intends to bring to an end, through a stroke of the pen, *first* our legal rights to be in West Berlin—and *secondly* our ability to make good on our commitment to the two million free people of that city. That we cannot permit.

We are clear about what must be done—and we intend to do it. I want to talk frankly with you tonight about the first steps that we shall take. These actions will require sacrifice on the part of many of our citizens. More will be required in the future. They will require, from all of us, courage and perseverance in the years to come. But if we and our allies act out of strength and unity of purpose—with calm determination and steady nerves—using restraint in our words as well as our weapons—I am hopeful that both peace and freedom will be sustained.

The immediate threat to free men is in West Berlin. But that isolated outpost is not an isolated problem. The threat is world-wide. Our effort must be equally wide and strong, and not be obsessed by any single manufactured crisis. We face a challenge in Berlin, but there is also a challenge in southeast

Asia, where the borders are less guarded, the enemy harder to find, and the danger of communism less apparent to those who have so little. We face a challenge in our hemisphere, and indeed wherever else the freedom of human beings is at stake.

Let me remind you that the fortunes of war and diplomacy left the free people of West Berlin in 1945 110 miles behind the Iron Curtain.

This map [shown for a few moments on the television screen] makes very clear the problem that we face. The white is West Germany—the East is the area controlled by the Soviet Union, and as you can see from the chart, West Berlin is 110 miles within the area which the Soviets now dominate—which is immediately controlled by the so-called East German regime.

We are there as a result of our victory over Nazi Germany—and our basic rights to be there deriving from that victory include both our presence in West Berlin and the enjoyment of access across East Germany. These rights have been repeatedly confirmed and recognized in special agreements with the Soviet Union. Berlin is not a part of East Germany, but a separate territory under the control of the allied powers. Thus our rights there are clear and deep-rooted. But in addition to those rights is our commitment to sustain—and defend, if need be—the opportunity for more than two million people to determine their own future and choose their own way of life.

II

Thus, our presence in West Berlin, and our access thereto, cannot be ended by any act of the Soviet government. The NATO shield was long ago extended to cover West Berlin—and we have given our word that an attack in that city will be regarded as an attack upon us all.

For West Berlin—lying exposed 110 miles inside East Germany, surrounded by Soviet troops and close to Soviet supply lines, has many roles. It is more than a showcase of liberty, a symbol, an island of freedom in a Communist sea. It is even more than a link with the Free World, a beacon of hope behind the Iron Curtain, an escape hatch for refugees.

West Berlin is all of that. But above all it has now become —as never before—the great testing place of Western courage and will, a focal point where our solemn commitments stretch-

ing back over the years since 1945, and Soviet ambitions now
meet in basic confrontation.

It would be a mistake for others to look upon Berlin, because
of its location, as a tempting target. The United States is there;
the United Kingdom and France are there; the pledge of NATO
is there—and the people of Berlin are there. It is as secure, in
that sense, as the rest of us—for we cannot separate its safety
from our own.

I hear it said that West Berlin is militarily untenable. And
so was Bastogne. And so, in fact, was Stalingrad. Any dangerous
spot is tenable if men—brave men will make it so.

We do not want to fight—but we have fought before. And
others in earlier times have made the same dangerous mistake
of assuming that the West was too selfish and too soft and too
divided to resist invasions of freedom in other lands. Those who
threaten to unleash the forces of war on a dispute over West
Berlin should recall the words of the ancient philosopher: "A
man who causes fear cannot be free from fear."

We cannot and will not permit the Communists to drive us
out of Berlin, either gradually or by force. For the fulfillment
of our pledge to that city is essential to the morale and security
of Western Germany, to the unity of Western Europe, and to the
faith of the entire Free World. Soviet strategy has long been
aimed, not merely at Berlin, but at dividing and neutralizing
all of Europe, forcing us back to our own shores. We must meet
our oft-stated pledge to the free peoples of West Berlin—and
maintain our rights and their safety, even in the face of force—
in order to maintain the confidence of other free peoples in our
word and our resolve. The strength of the alliance on which
our security depends is dependent in turn on our willingness to
meet our commitments to them.

III

So long as the Communists insist that they are preparing to
end by themselves unilaterally our rights in West Berlin and
our commitments to its people, we must be prepared to defend
those rights and those commitments. We will at all times be
ready to talk, if talk will help. But we must also be ready to
resist with force, if force is used upon us. Either alone would
fail. Together, they can serve the cause of freedom and peace.

The new preparations that we shall make to defend the peace are part of the long-term build-up in our strength which has been underway since January. They are based on our needs to meet a world-wide threat, on a basis which stretches far beyond the present Berlin crisis. Our primary purpose is neither propaganda nor provocation—but preparation.

A first need is to hasten progress toward the military goals which the North Atlantic allies have set for themselves. In Europe today nothing less will suffice. We will put even greater resources into fulfilling those goals, and we look to our allies to do the same.

The supplementary defense build-ups that I asked from the Congress in March and May have already started moving us toward these and our other defense goals. They included an increase in the size of the Marine Corps, improved readiness of our reserves, expansion of our air and sea lift, and stepped-up procurement of needed weapons, ammunition, and other items. To insure a continuing invulnerable capacity to deter or destroy any aggressor, they provided for the strengthening of our missile power and for putting 50 per cent of our B-52 and B-47 bombers on a ground alert which would send them on their way with fifteen minutes warning.

These measures must be speeded up, and still others must now be taken. We must have sea and air lift capable of moving our forces quickly and in large numbers to any part of the world.

But even more importantly, we need the capability of placing in any critical area at the appropriate time a force which, combined with those of our allies, is large enough to make clear our determination and our ability to defend our rights at all costs— and to meet all levels of aggressor pressure with whatever levels of force are required. We intend to have a wider choice than humiliation or all-out nuclear action.

While it is unwise at this time either to call up or send abroad excessive numbers of these troops before they are needed, let me make it clear that I intend to take, as time goes on, whatever steps are necessary to make certain that such forces can be deployed at the appropriate time without lessening our ability to meet our commitments elsewhere.

Thus, in the days and months ahead, I shall not hesitate to ask the Congress for additional measures, or exercise any of the executive powers that I possess to meet this threat to peace. Everything essential to the security of freedom must be done; and if that should require more men, or more taxes, or more controls, or other new powers, I shall not hesitate to ask them. The measures proposed today will be constantly studied, and altered as necessary. But while we will not let panic shape our policy, neither will we permit timidity to direct our program.

Accordingly, I am now taking the following steps:

1. I am tomorrow requesting the Congress for the current fiscal year an additional $3.247 billion of appropriations for the armed forces.

2. To fill out our present Army divisions, and to make more men available for prompt deployment, I am requesting an increase in the Army's total authorized strength from 875,000 to approximately 1 million men.

3. I am requesting an increase of 29,000 and 63,000 men respectively in the active duty strength of the Navy and the Air Force.

4. To fulfill these manpower needs, I am ordering that our draft calls be doubled and tripled in the coming months; I am asking the Congress for authority to order to active duty certain ready reserve units and individual reservists, and to extend tours of duty; and, under that authority, I am planning to order to active duty a number of air transport squadrons and Air National Guard tactical air squadrons, to give us the air-lift capacity and protection that we need. Other reserve forces will be called up when needed.

5. Many ships and planes once headed for retirement are to be retained or reactivated, increasing our air power tactically and our sea lift, air lift, and anti-submarine warfare capability. In addition, our strategic air power will be increased by delaying the deactivation of B-47 bombers.

6. Finally, some $1.8 billion—about half of the total sum— is needed for the procurement of non-nuclear weapons, ammunition and equipment.

The details on all these requests will be presented to the Congress tomorrow. Subsequent steps will be taken to suit subsequent needs. Comparable efforts for the common defense are being discussed with our NATO allies. For their commitment and interest are as precise as our own.

And let me add that I am well aware of the fact that many American families will bear the burden of these requests. Studies or careers will be interrupted; husbands and sons will be called away; incomes in some cases will be reduced. But these are burdens which must be borne if freedom is to be defended—Americans have willingly borne them before—and they will not flinch from the task now.

IV

We have another sober responsibility. To recognize the possibilities of nuclear war in the missile age, without our citizens knowing what they should do and where they should go if bombs begin to fall, would be a failure of responsibility. In May, I pledged a new start on civil defense. Last week, I assigned, on the recommendation of the Civil Defense Director, basic responsibility for this program to the Secretary of Defense, to make certain it is administered and coordinated with our continental defense efforts at the highest civilian level. Tomorrow, I am requesting of the Congress new funds for the following immediate objectives: to identify and mark space in existing structures—public and private—that could be used for fall-out shelters in case of attack; to stock those shelters with food, water, first-aid kits and other minimum essentials for survival; to increase their capacity; to improve our air-raid warning and fall-out detection systems, including a new household warning system which is now under development; and to take other measures that will be effective at an early date to save millions of lives if needed.

In the event of an attack, the lives of those families which are not hit in a nuclear blast and fire can still be saved—*if* they can be warned to take shelter and *if* that shelter is available. We owe that kind of insurance to our families—and to our country. In contrast to our friends in Europe, the need for this kind of protection is new to our shores. But the time to start is now. In the coming months, I hope to let every citizen know what steps he can take without delay to protect his family in case of attack. I know that you will want to do no less.

V

The addition of $207 million in civil defense appropriations brings our total new defense budget requests to $3.454 billion, and a total of $47.5 billion for the year. This is an increase in the defense budget of $6 billion since January, and has resulted in official estimates of a budget deficit of over $5 billion. The Secretary of the Treasury and other economic advisers assure me, however, that our economy has the capacity to bear this new request.

We are recovering strongly from this year's recession. The increase in this last quarter of our year of our total national output was greater than that for any postwar period of initial recovery. And yet, wholesale prices are actually lower than they were during the recession, and consumer prices are only $\frac{1}{4}$ of 1 per cent higher than they were last October. In fact, this last quarter was the first in eight years in which our production has increased without an increase in the over-all price index. And for the first time since the fall of 1959, our gold position has improved and the dollar is more respected abroad. These gains, it should be stressed, are being accomplished with budget deficits far smaller than those of the 1958 recession.

This improved business outlook means improved revenues; and I intend to submit to the Congress in January a budget for the next fiscal year which will be strictly in balance. Nevertheless, should an increase in taxes be needed—because of events in the next few months—to achieve that balance, or because of subsequent defense rises, those increased taxes will be requested in January.

Meanwhile, to help make certain that the current deficit is held to a safe level, we must keep down all expenditures not thoroughly justified in budget requests. The luxury of our current post-office deficit must be ended. Costs in military procurement will be closely scrutinized—and in this effort I welcome the cooperation of the Congress. The tax loopholes I have specified— on expense accounts, overseas income, dividends, interest, cooperatives and others—must be closed.

I realize that no public revenue measure is welcomed by everyone. But I am certain that every American wants to pay his fair share, and not leave the burden of defending freedom entirely to those who bear arms. For we have mortgaged our very future on this defense—and we cannot fail to meet our responsibility.

VI

But I must emphasize again that the choice is not merely between resistance and retreat, between atomic holocaust and surrender. Our peacetime military posture is traditionally defensive; but our diplomatic posture need not be. Our response to the Berlin crisis will not be merely military or negative. It will be more than merely standing firm. For we do not intend to leave it to others to choose and monopolize the forum and the framework of discussion. We do not intend to abandon our duty to mankind to seek a peaceful solution.

As signers of the UN Charter, we shall always be prepared to discuss international problems with any and all nations that are willing to talk—and listen—with reason. If they have proposals—not demands—we shall hear them. If they seek genuine understanding—not concessions of our rights—we shall meet with them. We have previously indicated our readiness to remove any actual irritants in West Berlin—but the freedom of that city is not negotiable. We cannot negotiate with those who say "What's mine is mine and what's yours is negotiable." But we are willing to consider any arrangement or treaty in Germany consistent with the maintenance of peace and freedom, and with the legitimate security interests of all nations.

We recognize the Soviet Union's historical concerns about their security in Central and Eastern Europe, after a series of ravaging invasions—and we believe arrangements can be worked out which will help to meet those concerns, and make it possible for both security and freedom to exist in this troubled area.

For it is not the freedom of West Berlin which is "abnormal" in Germany today, but the situation in that entire divided country. If anyone doubts the legality of our rights in Berlin, we are ready to have it submitted to international adjudication. If anyone doubts the extent to which our presence is desired by the people of West Berlin, compared to East German feelings about their regime, we are ready to have that question submitted to a free vote in Berlin and, if possible, among all the German people. And let us hear at that time from the two and one-half million refugees who have fled the Communist regime in East Germany—voting for Western-type freedom with their feet.

The world is not deceived by the Communist attempt to label Berlin as a hot-bed of war. There is peace in Berlin today.

The source of world trouble and tension is Moscow, not Berlin. And if war begins, it will have begun in Moscow and not Berlin.

For the choice of peace or war is largely theirs, not ours. It is the Soviets who have stirred up this crisis. It is they who are trying to force a change. It is they who have opposed free elections. It is they who have rejected an all-German peace treaty, and the rulings of international law. And as Americans know from our history on our own old frontier, gun battles are caused by outlaws, and not by officers of the peace.

In short, while we are ready to defend our interests, we shall also be ready to search for peace—in quiet exploratory talks— in formal or informal meetings. We do not want military considerations to dominate the thinking of either East or West. And Mr. Khrushchev may find that his invitation to other nations to join in a meaningless treaty may lead to *their* inviting *him* to join in the community of peaceful men, in abandoning the use of force, and in respecting the sanctity of agreements.

VII

While all of these efforts go on, we must not be diverted from our total responsibilities, from other dangers, from other tasks. If new threats in Berlin or elsewhere should cause us to weaken our program of assistance to the developing nations who are also under heavy pressure from the same source—or to halt our efforts for realistic disarmament—or to disrupt or slow down our economy—or to neglect the education of our children—then those threats will surely be the most successful and least costly maneuver in Communist history. For we can afford all these efforts, and more—but we cannot afford *not* to meet this challenge.

And the challenge is not to us alone. It is a challenge to every nation which asserts its sovereignty under a system of liberty. It is a challenge to all who want a world of free choice. It is a special challenge to the Atlantic Community—the heartland of human freedom.

We in the West must move together in building military strength. We must consult one another more closely than ever before. We must together design our proposals for peace, and labor together as they are pressed at the conference table. And together we must share the burdens and the risks of this effort.

The Atlantic Community, as we know it, has been built in response to challenge: the challenge of European chaos in 1947; of the Berlin blockade in 1948, the challenge of Communist aggression in Korea in 1950. Now, standing strong and prosperous, after an unprecedented decade of progress, the Atlantic Community will not forget either its history or the principles which gave it meaning.

The solemn vow each of us gave to West Berlin in time of peace will not be broken in time of danger. If we do not meet our commitments to Berlin, where will we later stand? If we are not true to our word there, all that we have achieved in collective security, which relies on these words, will mean nothing. And if there is one path above all others to war, it is the path of weakness and disunity.

Today, the endangered frontier of freedom runs through divided Berlin. We want it to remain a frontier of peace. This is the hope of every citizen of the Atlantic Community; every citizen of Eastern Europe; and, I am confident, every citizen of the Soviet Union. For I cannot believe that the Russian people— who bravely suffered enormous losses in the Second World War —would now wish to see the peace upset once more in Germany. The Soviet government alone can convert Berlin's frontier of peace into a pretext for war.

The steps I have indicated tonight are aimed at avoiding that war. To sum it all up: we seek peace—but we shall not surrender. That is the central meaning of this crisis—and the meaning of your Government's policy.

With your help, and the help of other free men, this crisis can be surmounted. Freedom can prevail—and peace can endure.

I would like to close with a personal word. When I ran for the presidency of the United States, I knew that this country faced serious challenges, but I could not realize—nor could any man realize who does not bear the burdens of this office—how heavy and constant would be those burdens.

Three times in my lifetime our country and Europe have been involved in major wars. In each case serious misjudgments were made on both sides of the intentions of others, which brought about great devastation.

Now, in the thermonuclear age, any misjudgment on either side about the intentions of the other could rain more devastation in several hours than has been wrought in all the wars of human history.

Therefore I, as President and Commander-in-Chief, and all of us as Americans, are moving through serious days. I shall bear this responsibility under our Constitution for the next three and one half years, but I am sure that we all, regardless of our occupations, will do our very best for our country, and for our cause. For all of us want to see our children grow up in a country at peace, and in a world where freedom endures.

I know that sometimes we get impatient, we wish for some immediate action that would end our perils. But I must tell you that there is no quick and easy solution. The Communists control over a billion people, and they recognize that if we should falter, their success would be imminent.

We must look to long days ahead, which if we are courageous and persevering can bring us what we all desire.

In these days and weeks I ask for your help, and your advice. I ask for your suggestions, when you think we could do better.

All of us I know love our country, and we shall all do our best to serve it.

In meeting my responsibilities in these coming months as President, I need your good will, and your support—and above all, your prayers.

THE UNDERLYING CRISIS: COERCION VS. CHOICE [3]

DEAN RUSK [4]

One of the vexing problems confronting the press and public officials is that of *context.* "It is almost never possible to give a complete
story on each of the events which arouse public interest." In an address
before the National Press Club in Washington, D.C., on July 10, 1961,
Secretary of State Dean Rusk underlined the dilemma which challenges
speakers and writers: "You [newsmen] and we [public officials] share
the difficulty of reducing complexities to manageable proportions and of
using accurately and economically the moments of attention we get from
a busy and preoccupied nation."

According to Secretary Rusk, citizens are prone to think of foreign
relations chiefly in terms of crises, large and small. This leads to dis-
tortion of context. It overlooks the many constructive relationships
which are constantly being established across national frontiers. Moreover, it fails to give "the sense of persistent underlying crisis." The
central issue of the underlying crisis, said the Secretary, "is the announced determination [by the Sino-Soviet empire] to impose a world
of coercion upon those not already subjected to it."

Secretary Rusk explained concisely the long-range policy of the
Administration to cope with this persistent emergency. This included
the strengthening of the United Nations and the Western community,
and the reassertion of the West's "leadership of the revolution of
political freedom" and the "revolution of economic and social progress."

According to the New York *Times,* one of the Secretary's associates
called this speech "pure Rusk." "Several drafts had been prepared for
him, but he put them aside and kept writing and rewriting almost
without interruption from yesterday morning until early this morning
[July 10]."

Following the address, newsmen engaged the Secretary in a ques-
tion-and-answer session.

Last year, as a private citizen, I had the temerity to give three
lectures on the conduct of our foreign relations. They dealt with
the roles of the President, the Secretary of State, and the Congress. The first was published; the other two, happily, were not.
The three were to make up a thin book—how thin I did not

[3] Text furnished by the Office of Public Services, Bureau of Public Affairs, Department of State, with permission for this reprint.

[4] For biographical note, see Appendix.

then appreciate. One matter which I underestimated was the problem of explaining foreign policy in a vigorous democracy, a democracy closely associated with more than forty allies and in friendly relations with more than fifty so-called "uncommitted nations," with, in the background, those also listening who would like to bring our democracy down.

Public officials are engaged in "in-service training," and I am grateful to many of you for your help—intended and unintended —with my education during these first months of office. I deeply believe that the public should be fully informed about the world situation and our courses of action to deal with it. In no other way can we mobilize both the necessary effort of a people who act through consent and the unity which is critically necessary in hazardous times. I believe, as well, that responsible public officials should in their statements seek to serve the public interest and not merely its passing curiosity. The public has a right to know, including the right to know that its serious business is being handled in a responsible fashion. For example, if there are differences between us and friendly nations about one or another aspect of the passing parade of events, these are more likely to be resolved by quiet conversation than by a public quarrel. If two of our friends find themselves in difficulty with each other, it is not always conducive to agreement for it to be publicly known that we have been offering friendly counsel.

And again, if a matter arises which is of deep concern to our allies and where unity among allies is critical to the sound handling of the issues involved, it is not always easy for the United States to sound off prematurely without consultation with those whose vital interests are also at stake.

But our policies are public, our purposes are those which the nation itself enjoins upon its government; in the main, our acts are public, because that is the way a democracy moves. But diplomacy cannot always be so, or else it would be little more than debate, adding its fuel to the very fires it hopes to quench.

The press and public officials have a common problem in presenting foreign policy issues to the American people. It is the problem of context. It arises in part because of the limitations of space and time limitations imposed upon both those who offer information and those who read or listen to it. It is almost never possible to give a complete story on each of the events which arouse public interest. You and we share the difficulty of reducing complexities to manageable proportions and of using accurately and economically the moments of attention we get from a busy and preoccupied nation.

We are accustomed to think of our foreign relations as a series of large or small crises. To do so is itself to distort out of context, for it overlooks the mass of constructive relationships which are steadily building across national frontiers and does not convey the sense of the persistent underlying crisis under which the world has lived since World War II.

Building a Decent World Order

As prelude to your questions, I should like to comment today on this underlying crisis from which many—but not all—of the troubles which attract our attention are derived.

Let us start from where we ourselves are and what we in this country should like to achieve in our relations with the rest of the world. Since World War II we have had more than one so-called great debate about foreign policy. Actually, the greatest debate of all occurred during that war, and the most eloquent voice was the war itself. Before the fighting was over we had concluded as a nation that we must throw ourselves into the building of a decent world order in which such conflagrations could not occur.

The nature of that world order was set forth succinctly in the Charter of the United Nations, a Charter backed by an overwhelming majority of the Senate and supported by an overwhelming majority of the nation. It called for a community of independent nations, each free to work out its own institutions as it saw fit but cooperating effectively and loyally with other nations on matters of common interest and concern. The inevitable disputes were to be settled by peaceful means; and let us not forget that the Charter supposed that the tried processes of negotiation, mediation, and adjudication were to be preferred over violent or fruitless debate. But parties in serious dispute were to seek the help of the broader international community in order that disinterested judgments could be brought to bear upon sensitive or inflamed issues.

As such a world order grew in strength and effectiveness, the limitation and reduction of arms would become possible, cooperation on economic and social problems would improve the lot of man, human rights would be strengthened, and the role of law would steadily take over from the law of the jungle. On matters of political arrangements, the underlying thesis was that the people themselves should play the decisive role as the principle of self-determination was brought to bear. It was then, and remains, our hope that man can take up once again the ancient aspirations of the race and move to free himself from the burdens of war, tyranny, and misery.

With deference to our shortcomings, I think it can be properly said that the United States threw itself with honesty and diligence into this great effort. It rapidly demobilized—more rapidly than events proved wise. It offered its atomic weapons to international control. It committed vast resources to the reconstruction of war-torn nations. It cooperated both in the large and in detail with the great cooperative ventures of the community of nations. Most important of all, it turned aside from the ambitions and appetites which have historically been associated with great power and conformed its national aims to those I have just described.

What Has Gone Wrong?

What has gone wrong? Why, after fifteen years, is there so much tension and danger in a world which had hoped for so much just yesterday? To be fair, let us not suppose that all of our problems are traceable to a single source. Under the best of conditions, the surging tides of nationalism and the insistent demands for economic and social improvement would have required great skill and understanding to handle the inevitable changes which were bound to come in our postwar world. But these were manageable, and there is no reason to suppose that they could not be accommodated in the processes of peaceful change.

The underlying crisis of our generation arises from the fact that the Soviet Union did not join the United Nations in fact, as well as in form, and lend itself to the commitments they and the rest of us made in the midst of a great war. The possession of power was transformed once more to ambition for more power.

The capacity to defy law became a contempt for law. Doctrines were revised and adapted to promote an imperialism as old as the tragic history of man. An entire people was sealed off from the rest of the world, and secrecy became a prime strategic weapon. The institutions of the international community were either ignored or undermined from within. The Soviet Union has just cast its ninety-fifth veto in the Security Council of the United Nations.

In the process the very language of international intercourse became distorted and contrived. "Peace" has become a word to describe whatever condition would promote their world revolution. "Aggression" is whatever stands in its way. "People's Democracy" is a term applied to regimes no one of which has been chosen by free election. Self-determination is loudly espoused but only in areas not under Communist control.

The normally attractive word "negotiation" is used as a weapon, for the only subjects to be negotiated are further concessions to Communist appetite. Agreements are offered but against the background of a long and sobering list of broken promises; an agreement is apparently a rest camp, where one pauses and refits for a further advance. New assurances are offered in the very act of withdrawing those earlier given. Law, as one of their spokesmen put it, "is like the tongue of a wagon—it goes in the direction in which it is pointed." And the gains of lawlessness are cited as the "new conditions" which justify new invasions of the rights of others.

Neutrality is temporary, a pasture growing green for future grazing. On January 6 Mr. Khrushchev said, "The revolutionary emergence of more and more peoples into the world arena creates exceptionally favorable conditions for an unprecedented broadening of the sphere of influence of Marxism-Leninism. The time is not far away when Marxism-Leninism will possess the minds of the majority of the world's population." Apparently, according to one of his homely maxims, "Every vegetable has its season."

Central Issue of the Crisis

The underlying crisis is not an ideological conflict between nineteenth century capitalism and nineteenth century Marxism. It does not result from a bilateral conflict between the Soviet Union and the United States.

The central issue of the crisis is the announced determination
to impose a world of coercion upon those not already subjected
to it. If this seems exaggerated simplicity, let us not be misled
by our own reluctance to believe what they say, for on this point
they have proved that they mean it. At stake is the survival and
growth of the world of free choice and of the free cooperation
pledged in the Charter. There is no "troika" on this issue—it is
posed between the Sino-Soviet empire and all the rest, whether
allied or neutral; and it is now posed in every continent.

The underlying crisis has shown itself in many forms—from
the cynical disregard of the pledges on liberated areas, made at
Yalta, to the latest threats to West Berlin. The calendar of
conflict between these two dates is filled with unceasing attempts
to expand an empire—some successful but many repelled by
those determined to be free.

Strengthening Western Solidarity

President Kennedy has taken up his great task with a deep
awareness of the nature of the crisis and of the actions required
by the continuing struggle for freedom.

It is essential to get on with the building of the world community designed by the Charter. This we would do in any event;
but it is here that the breadth and depth of the crisis are fully
revealed, and it is here that those who would not be coerced
can act together for a world of peace. We speak of uncommitted
nations, and we usually mean those who are committed to
neither of the principal blocs on the present scene. But all
nations have commitments arising out of their own interests and
out of their own hopes for the future. In the United Nations
commitments to the Charter can weave the fabric of common
interest which, by reaching beyond the cold war, may determine
its outcome.

No less essential is the strengthening of the solidarity of
NATO and of the Western Community—possessed of enormous
capacity to shape the course of events. The political, economic,
and military strengthening of the Western Community is an
urgent matter to which the Administration is giving full attention. The President has also seen that the Western world must
recapture the leadership of its own revolution of political free-

dom. It is a revolution which the West itself has taken into every continent and which continues to stir men to action. This struggle for freedom in the West itself was not painless; nor will it be in other places in our own time. But we dare not yield its leadership to those who would seize it, subvert it, and use it to destroy us.

The President is also asking us, and other economically advanced free nations, to reassert our leadership of the revolution of economic and social progress. The world of coercion is offering tempting bait for those who are determined to shake off their misery and want. We believe that freedom and progress are historic partners and that the alleged choice between rapid progress and free institutions is false. But this we must prove. This is the meaning of the President's Alliance for Progress, which is stirring the hopes and the hard thinking of the nations of our own hemisphere. This is the meaning of the rapidly growing effort of the Western Community to throw substantial resources behind the economic and social development of less favored nations. This is why the President is asking for thoughtful planning, effective leadership, and determined self-help from those who need external assistance for national growth. And this is why the President is asking the Congress for aid legislation and appropriations which will put us in a position to help generate the momentum of development—aid which must be provided, in association with others, in the amounts and for the periods of time required to achieve enduring and satisfying results.

During these first months the President has established direct contact with the leadership of many nations in order to give us as quickly as possible an accurate understanding of their interests and views. In his own discussions with them, through the Vice President, Ambassador [Adlai E.] Stevenson, and others, he has been able to lay the basis for the greater unity of our several alliances and the greater effort which will be required to deal with the continuing crisis.

The President has recognized the changes which are occurring in the strategic problems which we and our allies must face and is moving, in consultation with other governments, to bring the free world's capabilities up to the needs of the variety of dangers which have to be confronted.

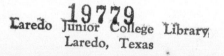

Effort To Relieve Arms Race

Despite the continuing crisis, we have felt it necessary to work diligently and realistically at the possibilities of disarmament. Even though the political atmosphere is not encouraging, an imaginative effort must be made to relieve the tensions arising from the arms race itself. We cannot understand how the Soviet Union, which has expended so much eloquence on disarmament, could have rejected the reasonable and workable treaty for the ban of nuclear testing which was tabled at Geneva this spring. "General and complete disarmament" are apparently among those words given a special meaning in the glossary of their world revolution. For reasonable people would suppose that the way to get there is to start and that the steps along the way must be such as to leave no one, in Aristide Briand's words, as "dupes or victims." Nevertheless our work goes forward, and we earnestly hope that the Congress will support the recent proposals of the President to make it effective.

Let me conclude by saying that the agenda of our foreign relations is filled with problems requiring and getting urgent attention. If there are those looking for still waters, we are not yet there. We can move on with confidence if we are prepared to do what has to be done. The free world has enormous strength, including the inner strength of purposes which are deeply rooted in the nature of man.

The world of coercion has its problems too. Dissensions within its ranks, national resistance to this modern imperialism, and a growing demand for freedom are among them. It has learned that economic aid does not buy puppets, that intimidation awakens its own resistance, that the United Nations is tougher than it thought, and that those who set out to "possess the minds" of man have set themselves against the course of history.

Our democracy must have its turbulent debate. Free nations will, of course, differ among themselves as they move to build a common interest out of disparate circumstance and varied responsibility. But the underlying crisis is becoming more widely understood, and out of it will come the responses which men must make when their freedom is at stake.

AN ADDRESS TO THE UNITED STATES SENATE [5]

MARGARET CHASE SMITH [6]

The First Session of the Eighty-seventh Congress was long, running from January 3 through September 26, 1961. Near the close of the Session, on September 21, Margaret Chase Smith, senior Senator (Republican) from Maine, made one of her infrequent addresses to the Senate, and, even more specifically, to the American people and President Kennedy. In a simple, forthright expression Senator Smith asked whether America had the *will and purpose* to stand up to Premier Khrushchev's repeated threats and demands. Why, she inquired, has American leadership permitted him to go on his reckless way with little more than token verbal resistance? Are we opposing willfully and firmly Premier Khrushchev's claim that the future belongs to the Communists?

These questions do not yield to easy answers. And Senator Smith did not profess to have the revealed truth. She believed, however, that Premier Khrushchev's bold actions were virtually encouraged by our announced reliance upon conventional rather than nuclear weapons:

> I would be the first to urge great caution; but I would also be the first to urge great firmness, and the last to cease opposing the submission of the unlimited interests of 180 million Americans to the stupidity of limited deterrence. . . .

> We have the nuclear capability—and he [Khrushchev] knows and fears it. But we have practically told him we do not have the will to use that one power with which we can stop him. *In short, we have the nuclear capability—but not the nuclear credibility.*

Senator Smith's words were clearly intended for American, not Russian, ears. But the message did not go unnoticed abroad. Premier Khrushchev found little in it to praise. According to a news report, he called the speech "a malicious man-hating call; . . . in her hatred of everything new and progressive [she] has decided to beat all records of savagery." An Associated Press dispatch of October 13 quoted Senator Smith as saying: "Mr. Khrushchev isn't really mad at me. I am not that important. He is angry because American officials have grown more firm since my speech September 21."

---

[5] Text furnished by Senator Smith, with permission for this reprint.

[6] For biographical note, see Appendix.

Some observers have labeled this speech a "Declaration of Courage," thus associating it with her "Declaration of Conscience," delivered to the United States Senate on June 1, 1950.

Senator Smith has been elected to three full terms in the Senate—a record held by no other woman. Her independence of thought and fidelity to duty have often been attested to by members on both sides of the aisle. On June 15, 1961, special tribute was paid her on the occasion of her completing the thousandth consecutive roll call in the Senate. In his statement of appreciation, Senator George D. Aiken (Republican, Vermont) expressed the hope "that she will not try to add another thousand to her consecutive votes. If I were she, I would take time off and miss twenty in succession and simply have a vacation." To which Senator Mike Mansfield (Democrat, Montana) replied: "I join the senior Senator from Vermont in expressing the hope that occasionally Senator Smith will play hooky from now on."

What I am about to say is addressed not only to the members of the United States Senate but to all Americans—and most specifically to the President of the United States.

Many times during the last decade or more we have been able to draw comfort from knowing we had strength and will that could command the world's respect and deter the Communists. But recent history is not reassuring. Ominous signs plague us.

Everywhere the Communists press forward stronger. Khrushchev, vowing to take over the world for communism, and acting with all the confidence of a winner, threatens to put an end to civilized survival for the world if we do not let him have his way.

In an effort to generate global enthusiasm for submission he has stained the sky and polluted the air with nuclear bursts.

At the dividing line in Berlin he has dared to make a frontal attack on freedom.

In speaking of the future he has embraced the risks of dire threats and ultimatums.

It is a grim spectacle such as we have never seen.

My purpose in asking your attention today is not to emphasize that this is a time of corroding fears and tensions.

You know this as well as I do.

It is not to suggest that I have some special talent which permits me to see clearly the way out of the never-never land between high hope and deep despair, into which we have wandered. That would be presumptuous of me; but although we do not yet know a way out, I am sure the time has come to *find a way out,* and to go once again to the high ground we enjoyed just a short time ago.

My purpose is not to recite our list of losses in the great conflict with world communism.

Being a long list, it is painfully evident, not only to us but to the rest of the world; and its implications are frightening.

My purpose is not to recite facts that all of us know well enough, but to pose a vital question, the answers for which *none* of us yet knows well enough. Not a question that I have composed, but which suggests itself. Not a question of selfish or parochial origin. But one far more important. A question of national interest.

The question for which I urge your attention is spawned from the ugly union of communism's unswerving ambition and its unscrupulous methods.

The implications of this question have put a chill into the hearts of millions who yearn for peace, yet it is spoken by few of us.

It now demands our attention.

While we still have time we must examine it to its deepest foundations, its remotest associations.

We must do this now.

If we fail to do it now, we may not be free to do it later on.

It is a question that challenges us to merciless objectivity and realism.

It is a challenge that is addressed not only to us who are here today. It is addressed to every American; in fact, to every free man and woman—and to every person who yearns to know what freedom is, or to regain a freedom wrested from him by force, or lost to him by inaction or bad advice.

What we learn from our examination, what we do about it— or *fail* to do—may be the difference for us between peace or war, win or lose, fear or freedom, and perhaps even life or death.

We must look at it against the backdrop of Khrushchev's reckless confidence, against the foul clouds of his nuclear blackmail blasts; then we can see the question I am about to pose to you as the most crucial the American people have faced since the Declaration of Independence launched us as the United States into the world of nations—not the strongest, not the largest; but nevertheless confident, firm and fearing no one.

The question which is posed to all of us, the question for which we *must* find the right answers across the board—realistically and urgently—is this:

What has happened that permits Khrushchev to act as he does?

Let me repeat:

What has happened that lets him do it?

Understand me, please. Not what is he *doing*. We know that only too well. Our national honor bears the scars and stains of what he is doing now and has done in the past. And he has warned us, arrogantly, of what he intends to do in the future, which is even worse.

These things we know.

But today—now—why does he feel free to do as he does? *Why?*

This also we must know. And if we do not know, we are likely to lose all control over shaping our future. Worse, we may lose our future itself.

We have been exhorted to have the moral courage to live with continuing conflict. No true American will argue otherwise, nor doubt that we are equal to the rigors of our moment in history. But let us also make sure we have the courage to go straight to the reasons *why* the conflict so often runs against us and burdens us so heavily, why Khrushchev so often has the initiative and we are satisfied only to *react.*

I sense a tendency, strange to the American character in world affairs, to retreat from circumstances rather than to face up to them realistically and master them. I am greatly disturbed by it. I am sure we can assume that Khrushchev is greatly pleased by it.

So let us here and now make a start on our examination of the question I have posed, by asking a related question:

Is Khrushchev free to act as he does because the Soviets have *suddenly* gained the over-all military advantage?

I say no.

The primary determinant for over-all military advantage today is the capacity for total nuclear war.

No matter how fervently Khrushchev, we, the non-aligneds, or anyone else would like to make it different, this is an inescapable fact and we must face it firmly and deal with it realistically.

No matter what the immediate objectives may be, no matter in what circumstances a critical conflict situation might develop, it is the capacity which both of us—the United States and the U.S.S.R.—must put into the scales first. And until the day comes when there is much more faith and good will in the world than there is today, it will invariably be the weight which tips the scales one way or the other—for us or against us—toward winning or losing; toward resoluteness or retreat; toward firmness or passivity; toward strength or submission.

It is generally agreed that as of today the over-all military advantage rests with us and our allies. We may be sure the Soviets also recognize this fact. When they undertake to assess their risks in any venture that they contemplate—Berlin, Laos, Africa, the Middle East, Cuba—they must begin at the top, with that for which their fears are greatest and their chances smallest. It is as true for them as it is for us that they cannot hide from realism.

All of us rightly fear that the conflict may go to the ultimate level of total nuclear war. No one can say whether or not this is the destiny of our generation. God grant that it is not. None can doubt that we are in grave danger, but this I feel strongly:

We are, as the President has said, engaged in a contest of will and purpose as well as force and violence.

If today, and in the days immediately ahead, we *fail* to meet the Soviets at the ultimate levels of *will and purpose,* the danger will be greatly widened that we will have no choice later on but to meet them at the ultimate levels of *force and violence*; either that or submit to their will. How much farther do you think Khrushchev would go today, how much faster would he move, if he was confident the over-all military advantage was on his side and not ours? if he did not have to worry about the risk of acting dangerously without having the over-all military advantage?

Let me say it again:

The over-all military advantage is on our side. But the day we lose sight of this fact, we are in danger of frightening ourselves, of being mesmerized by Khrushchev's confidence and *deterring ourselves* instead of deterring the Soviets. While we are concerned with all that might happen to us, we must never forget that *Khrushchev also has reason to be afraid; and the main reason is plain*:

There is a grim prospect indeed for a postwar U.S.S.R. stripped of its strength and reduced to a third- or fourth-rate nation, even though in the process of losing it he has wrought great damage on us. This is the *choice he* must face.

To say that the Kremlin's risks are great does not make our own risks less. But it does encourage perspective and this is important.

The risks run both ways. This is not enough to eliminate the conflict. I believe the Communists will always go as far and as fast as we indicate we will permit them to go. But it does create an environment in which our deterrence can be effective, if we are firm enough, if our will and purpose are equal to the test.

I am disturbed that there are some who say, in effect, we can do *more* in deterring the Soviets by preparing to do *less* against them if they should provoke armed hostilities. I refer specifically to the highly articulate and persuasive zealots who argue that increasing conventional forces is the best way to create more effective deterrence. They believe that flexibility in the application of military force can come only from conventional forces.

I know of nothing in political or military history which supports a thesis that it is safer to be weak than strong.

Until the Soviets change their ways and join the society of respectable nations, I see no hope of deterring them by making the risks they must face *less fearful* for them.

I know of no reason why we should be driven to a concept which—no matter how it is phrased—means that in order to prove our determination we would risk sacrificing the lives of men in the battle line rather than risk holding the enemy against the prospect that is most fearful to him.

That is a weak choice of risks for the strongest people in the world.

What is the origin of this fear of risks? It is not part of our heritage.

The greatness of this country was not won by people who were afraid of risks. It was won for us by men and women with little physical power at their command who nevertheless were willing to submit to risks. Could it not be lost for us by people with great physical power at their command but nevertheless willing to risk submitting? I believe it could.

So may I plead once more for perspective. Nothing has happened which suddenly has transferred the power of the over-all military advantage from us to the Soviets. *We can defeat the U.S.S.R. at any intensity of armed conflict unless we have degraded our fighting capacity greatly by self-imposed restrictions, such as restrictions on the use of tactical nuclear weapons.*

Our words concerning early use of tactical nuclear weapons if required can be invalidated quickly if our actions demonstrate that our major efforts and investments in time of great peril such as now, are directed mainly towards increases in conventional forces.

Mr. President, brave words are fine—but action speaks louder than words and deters Khrushchev much more.

We have the military basis for clearly demonstrating our will and purpose—for making deterrence work. But we will never deter the Soviets by backing away, or by offering to fight *on their terms* because we are fearful of provoking them by indicating beyond all doubt that we will fight, if fight we must, on *our terms.*

I would be the first to urge great caution; but I would also be the first to urge great firmness, and the last to cease opposing the submission of the unlimited interests of 180 million Americans to the stupidity of limited deterrence. There are other countries, once free, that have learned too late that the ultimate cost of partial security can be total defeat, or subjugation.

I repeat that it is not military strength *suddenly* acquired by the Soviets which permits Khrushchev to act as he does.

Is it then that our own military strength has suddenly deteriorated?

Have we been *suddenly* weakened?

Again I say no.

Every military authority presently responsible for our military posture will attest that our forces are stronger, not weaker; more alerted and ready, not *less* prepared.

We cannot conclude that *this* gives Khrushchev cause for his reckless confidence. He has not *won* the military advantage from us, and it has not *accrued* to him through our own military deficiencies.

So we must go further and ask yet another question:

Is it conceivable that Khrushchev could assess that the will of the American people has collapsed? That we are ready to submit? That he can win with blackmail? That Americans as the saying goes would rather be *red* than dead?

How do you respond to a question as impossible as this?

And yet it must be asked, for, as I have said, we must examine the fundamental question I have posed to its deepest foundations.

What has happened that permits Khrushchev to act as he does?

What gives Khrushchev his ticket to such great confidence?

What does he assess about us that makes him so sure?

What have we indicated to him that causes him to be so arrogant—to take such *wide risks,* in our view, in going so far?

If we hold the military advantage, why, you may well ask, is our deterrence not more effective? What's the reason it is not?

The reason is that deterrence is not a matter of forces and fire power alone. The restraints and influence are projected from the capacity to accomplish a purpose; *not just from what we have but from what we will do.*

Deterrence cannot be regarded as an assured fact. It is a sensitive condition, always subject to proof.

Nevertheless there are influential advocates of the so-called stable deterrence.

I believe such proposals to be, at worst, demonstrably false and, at best, highly questionable.

We are dealing with military power on both sides that is infinitely complicated, composed of many critical elements. This power itself floats on a sea of uncertainty, constantly subject to the restless tides of progress and the tidal waves of great change. *To say that we can count on achieving and maintaining a balance or stability in these conditions—even if we had the Soviet's cooperation, much less their opposition—is nothing short of wishful thinking—a form of "nuclear escapism" to dodge the hard, cold facts.*

I am frightened by inferences that we can get rid of the nuclear peril by this device of sweeping it under the rug. I fear it would trip us and catch us off balance sooner or later.

We must examine yet another facet of this critical situation, namely, what is it that Khrushchev most likely assesses from what our spokesmen say, in the context of what we do and fail to do?

What are the measures that we have taken to convince him, and the rest of the world, of our will and purpose?

What kind of raw material have we provided for Khrushchev to analyze, study, assess and use as a basis for his conclusions and actions?

I recall some of the inspiring words of the President's inaugural address, as our nation turned with high hopes toward this year 1961. Specifically:

> To those nations which would make themselves our adversary, we offer not a pledge but a request: that both sides begin anew the quest for peace, before the dark powers of destruction unleashed by science engulf all humanity in planned or accidental self-destruction.
> We dare not tempt them with weakness. For only when our arms are sufficient beyond doubt can we be certain beyond doubt that they will never be employed.

As I see the dark clouds that now hang low over the new frontiers of hope toward which the attention of Americans and the rest of the world was directed on that day, I wonder what it is that has tempted Castro to stoke the fires of hatred still higher in his communized Cuba and to challenge United States strength and influence throughout Latin America.

I do not *know* what Castro thinks; but I doubt that he has been *tempted* by a *high* assessment of our *will and purpose*.

Like millions of Americans, I was deeply impressed with the President, when, in his televised press conference, he pointed to a map and eloquently explained why we had to stand firm on Laos.

The words were brave and inspiring—but only to be followed by no brave action to back up those words.

As I see the perils that press in on us, I wonder what it is that impelled Khrushchev to choose the moment of his return from his Vienna meeting with the President to fling into the face of the American people his ultimatum on a treaty with East Germany and thereafter to bring on the Berlin crisis.

I do not *know* what Khrushchev thinks; but I cannot believe that he has been *tempted* in his Berlin gamble by a *high* assessment of our *will and purpose*.

Neither can we know how many others wonder about the course of events in much the same way as I do. But that there *are* others we do know; and I quote one now: Mr. Chalmers Roberts, in the Washington *Post* recently:

> Power and willingness to use it are fundamental to great nations. That the United States has the power is not doubted in Moscow, by every sign available here. But Khrushchev's latest actions indicate that he doubts the President's willingness to use it.
>
> And so it now appears that Khrushchev has decided to take the world to the brink for a test of will on the outcome of which may depend the future not only of West Berlin but the freedom of mankind.

We have a decided nuclear capability advantage over Khrushchev—and he knows it. Otherwise he wouldn't have resumed nuclear tests and would not have been deterred in the past in the slightest.

But he is confident we won't use it for he sees us turning to emphasis on conventional weapons—and ironically he has an obviously great superiority in conventional weapons and manpower over us.

We have in effect played into his hands—for the kind of warfare in which he knows he can beat us. We have restricted ourselves on the freedom of choice to use the nuclear tactical weapons which he knows would defeat him if he started war.

In short, we have the nuclear capability—and he knows and fears it. But we have practically told him we do not have the will to use that one power with which we can stop him.

In short, we have the nuclear capability—but not the nuclear credibility.

I recall some of the ringing words by the President in his address to the nation last July.

Specifically: "We cannot and will not permit the Communists to drive us out of Berlin, either gradually or by force."

I cannot know what Khrushchev thinks, what it is that influences him, what he looks for when he makes his judgments;

but I fervently hope that he would not make his final assessment as to our will and purpose in Berlin on the basis of what he has seen and deduced from, for example, Laos and Cuba.

God forbid that the pattern of brave words on Laos and Cuba followed by no brave action be repeated on Berlin.

As fervently as I hope Khrushchev *would not* be influenced unduly by what he might assess from the record in Laos and Cuba, I hope with even greater fervency that he *would* recall other times and other places, where American strength and American will have prevailed in American purpose. For example:

Lebanon, in 1958, where we acted promptly and unequivocally to prevent the threatened overthrow of a government friendly to us.

Admittedly, no one can know what might have happened if our forces had not been sent promptly to the scene. *But everyone knows what did happen after they were sent there. The threatened trouble dissolved.*

Or the Berlin airlift of 1948-1949, through which the Soviets' first major effort to force us out of Berlin was defeated—admittedly under circumstances different from those we face today, but nevertheless by firm and prompt action under the same principles to which we are dedicated today.

Or the off-shore islands in the Straits of Formosa, where long ago our firmness was proved to the Communists beyond doubt.

I am thankful that we have such examples of will and purpose to balance the record in some degree at this vital time—when we can be sure that every indication of our determination or lack of it is submitted to the most critical of examinations in Moscow; when a miscalculation in this respect by Moscow could bring on the greatest calamity since the first day of the recorded history of mankind.

Last April, when the American Society of Newspaper Editors met in Washington, the President beautifully phrased his address to them. Referring to events associated with Castro's Cuba, he said he wanted the record to show that "our restraint is not inexhaustible."

I not only agree wholeheartedly with the President in this reflection of our feelings, but I urge that we apply the same thought most seriously in other vital considerations, because:

Neither is our deterrent capacity inexhaustible. It must be revitalized appropriately with actions as well as with words and military forces.

Neither can we afford to assume that the confidence of the American people is inexhaustible. We cannot expect the national will to overcome forever the enervating effects of repeated losses without its being revitalized by the new strength of meaningful victories.

I am confident that we *can* do better.

I believe with all my heart that we *can* win our objectives.

These are the reasons why I speak as I do today in appealing to all Americans—and especially to the President of the United States on the eve of his address to a United Nations that is threatened with collapse for lack of will and determination.

These are the reasons why I could not take myself away from the Senate Chamber and go back to the people whose trust I hold without making my concern known, without asking:

How much longer can we afford to lose? When will we start to win?

Where will we draw the line?

If we fail to stand firm in Berlin—if we fail to stand there with the *best we have,* where in the world will we draw the line?

In the name of the courage, determination and sacrifices of our forebears, *let us not be afraid to be right at this critical time.*

General de Gaulle made a statement in his press conference on September 6, 1961, which the leaders of the West could well consider because it exemplifies the realism and the determination that is so desperately needed. I place it in the *Record* at this point of my remarks and I invite your study of it.

One may well ask why the Soviets suddenly took the pretext of Berlin to demand that the status of the city be changed—willingly or by force. One may ask, too, why the situation in Berlin, which for sixteen years seemed tolerable to them, and which they themselves created with the United States and Great Britain at the Potsdam conference—at which France was not present—*now, suddenly, seems intolerable.* One may ask why they are suddenly coupling their demands with frightful threats. One may ask whether anyone really believes that the German Federal Republic, as it is, is today a threat to Russia. One may ask whether there is any Russian who believes this, since the Kremlin claims that they are in a position to crush totally and immediately, with bombs equivalent apparently to over 100 million tons of TNT, anyone who lifts a hand against the Communist world.

There is in all this welter of imprecations and cries organized by the Soviets so much that is arbitrary and artificial that one is led to attribute it either to the premeditated unleashing of wild ambitions or regard it as an attempt to conceal great difficulties. The second hypothesis seems to me the more plausible because, despite the constraint, isolation, and violent acts to which the Communists have shackled the countries under their yoke, and despite certain collective successes which they have achieved by exerting pressure on the majority of their subjects, in fact, communism's shortcomings, its defiances, its domestic failures, and on top of it all, its character of inhuman oppression, are being felt more and more by the elite and the masses.

The Communists are less and less able to delude and to curb. And then also the satellites, which the Soviet regime holds under its laws, are experiencing more and more, because of national feelings, all that is cruel in the annexation which they have suffered.

Thus, one can understand that in these conditions the Soviets consider the Berlin affair an appropriate occasion for distracting the attention of their own people and others. And, in fact, with Berlin where it is, it will be relatively easy for them to demonstrate on the spot, that the restrictive measures which they have taken have for them limited risks.

And then, they may think that the United States, England, and France will allow themselves to slide into discouragement, into resignation, and thus the withdrawal of these three powers would be a hard blow to the Atlantic alliance. Moreover, the whole world would be shown that the totalitarian regime—the totalitarian camp—is decidedly the stronger in the face of an uncertain and divided West.

But, to be precise, this is not true. Of course the Soviets have at their disposal terrible nuclear arms, but the West has formidable ones too. If a world conflict were to break out, the use of these forces of destruction would doubtless bring in its wake, in particular, the complete overthrow of Russia and of countries under the Communist yoke. What is the use of ruling over dead men? And, moreover, the rule would itself be finished, for in such a disaster the backbone of the regime would be broken as well—the backbone of a regime which rules only with an authoritarian apparatus and the police, with everything rigidly planned and implacably enforced. This the Soviet leaders know in spite of all their boasting.

The Western powers have, then, no reason for not considering the Soviet moves with a clear eye and a firm heart.

It is true, I repeat, that locally, in Berlin, the act of force which would be involved might provoke, might procure for the Soviets certain advantages, since it would obviously be difficult for the Western powers to act from a distance on the territory and in the air of the former German capital. However, the West could answer very well on the seas and in the skies crossed by Soviet ships and planes, and this would be far from their bases. This poor exchange would undoubtedly not end to the advantage of the Soviets. In short, if the latter wants to reduce the positions and cut the communications of the Allies in Berlin by force, the Allies must maintain their positions and their communications by force. Certainly one thing leads to another, as they say, and if all this leads to a multiplication of the hostile acts of the Soviets, acts which must be answered, it may end in general war. But it would be because the Soviets deliberately wished it, and in that case any preliminary retreat by the West would only have served to enfeeble and divide it without preventing the outcome.

At a certain point in facing the threats of an ambitious imperialism, any retreat has the effect of overexciting the aggressor, of encouraging him to double his pressure, and, finally, facilitates and hastens his attack. In summation, the Western powers have at present no better means of serving world peace than remaining firm and direct.

I urge the President of the United States to consider these thoughts I have expressed before he makes his address to the United Nations Assembly.

While I agree with him that we should not negotiate from fear or fear to negotiate—I say we should not fear to refuse to negotiate on any matter that is not negotiable.

In these perilous hours, I fear that the American people are ahead of their leaders in realism and courage—but behind them in knowledge of the facts because the facts have not been given to them.

I would hope that every American would read what I have said today and would express themselves by direct correspondence to the President.

"LET US CALL A TRUCE TO TERROR" [7]

JOHN F. KENNEDY [8]

"There are moments in history when words can make a vital difference." Such a moment, in the opinion of the editors of the *Saturday Review*, came on September 25, 1961, when President Kennedy spoke before the sixteenth General Assembly of the United Nations. The occasion was somber, not unlike that which prompted President Eisenhower a year previously to come before the world organization. At stake was the fate of the United Nations—the institution that Adlai E. Stevenson has called the "listening post of the human race." And the leader of the free world had an obligation to speak out for it.

In his first major policy speech before the United Nations, the President met head-on the Soviet proposal for a tripartite division of authority in the organization. The death of Secretary-General Dag Hammarskjold had given the Soviet Union the long-sought opportunity to change the character of the United Nations. Its "troika" plan would make the Secretariat a three-man authority composed of representatives from the Soviet Union, the Western bloc, and the neutralist group. Each would have the veto power.

To this plan the President replied:

> However difficult it may be to fill Mr. Hammarskjold's place, it can better be filled by one man rather than by three. Even the three horses of the troika did not have three drivers, all going in different directions. They had only one—and so must the United Nations executive. To install a triumvirate, or any rotating authority, in the United Nations administrative offices would replace order with anarchy, action with paralysis, and confidence with confusion.

Mr. Kennedy restated the American position on the Berlin crisis and on the continuing threats in southeast Asia. Occupying a central position in his speech, however, was the outline of a bold disarmament plan which would eventually remove the weapons of annihilation from all countries, and strengthen the United Nations' machinery for settling disputes. A document explaining the complete *Program for General and Complete Disarmament in a Peaceful World* was introduced at the General Assembly after the President's speech. On April 18, 1962, Arthur H. Dean, head of the United States delegation,

[7] Text furnished by Pierre Salinger, press secretary to the President, with permission for this reprint.

[8] For biographical note, see **Appendix.**

submitted the specific details of this proposal to the seventeen-nation disarmament conference meeting at Geneva.

Through United Nations radio and the Voice of America the President's speech was broadcast throughout the world. The response was generally enthusiastic. Although Andrei A. Gromyko, Soviet Foreign Minister, did not applaud the address, even he was reported as saying that the President was in "good form." Which, indeed, he was. Clearly, firmly, but without a trace of belligerence, he pledged the country's adherence to a strong United Nations and challenged the Soviet Union to a *peace race*—"to advance together, step by step, stage by stage, until general and complete disarmament has been achieved."

We meet in an hour of grief and challenge. Dag Hammarskjold is dead. But the United Nations lives. His tragedy is deep in our hearts, but the task for which he died is at the top of our agenda. A noble servant of peace is gone. But the quest for peace lies before us.

The problem is not the death of one man—the problem is the life of this organization. It will either grow to meet the challenge of our age—or it will be gone with the wind, without influence, without force, without respect. Were we to let it die— to enfeeble its vigor—to cripple its powers—we would condemn the future.

For in the development of this organization rests the only true alternative to war—and war appeals no longer as a rational alternative. Unconditional war can no longer lead to unconditional victory. It can no longer serve to settle disputes. It can no longer concern the great powers alone. For a nuclear disaster, spread by winds and waters and fear, could well engulf the great and the small, the rich and the poor, the committed and the uncommitted alike. Mankind must put an end to war— or war will put an end to mankind.

So let us here resolve that Dag Hammarskjold did not live— or die—in vain. Let us call a truce to terror. Let us invoke the blessings of peace. And, as we build an international capacity to keep peace, let us join in dismantling the national capacity to wage war.

II

This will require new strength and new roles for the United Nations. For disarmament without checks is but a shadow— and a community without law is but a shell. Already the United

Nations has become both the measure and the vehicle of man's most generous impulses. Already it has provided—in the Middle East, in Asia, in Africa this year in the Congo—a means of holding violence within bounds.

But the great question which confronted this body in 1945 is still before us—whether man's cherished hopes for progress and peace are to be destroyed by terror and disruption—whether the "foul winds of war" can be tamed in time to free the cooling winds of reason—and whether the pledges of our Charter are to be fulfilled or defied: pledges to secure peace, progress, human rights and world law.

In this hall, there are not three forces, but two. One is composed of those who are trying to build the kind of world described in Articles I and II of the Charter. The other, seeking a far different world, would undermine this organization in the process.

Today of all days our dedication to the Charter must be maintained. It must be strengthened first of all, by the selection of an outstanding civil servant to carry forward the responsibilities of the Secretary-General—a man endowed with both the wisdom and the power to make meaningful the moral force of the world community. The late Secretary-General nurtured and sharpened the United Nations' obligation to act. But he did not invent it. It was there in the Charter. It is still there in the Charter.

However difficult it may be to fill Mr. Hammarskjold's place, it can better be filled by one man rather than by three. Even the three horses of the troika did not have three drivers, all going in different directions. They had only one—and so must the United Nations executive. To install a triumvirate, or any rotating authority, in the United Nations administrative offices would replace order with anarchy, action with paralysis, and confidence with confusion.

The Secretary-General, in a very real sense, is the servant of the General Assembly. Diminish his authority and you diminish the authority of the only body where all nations, regardless of power, are equal and sovereign. Until all the powerful are just, the weak will be secure only in the strength of this Assembly.

Effective and independent executive action is not the same question as balanced representation. In view of the enormous change in membership in this body since its founding, the

American delegation will join in any effort for the prompt review and revision of the composition of United Nations bodies.

But to give this organization three drivers—to permit each great power to decide its own case—would entrench the cold war in the headquarters of peace. Whatever advantages such a plan may hold out to my own country, as one of the great powers, we reject it. For we far prefer world law, in the age of self-determination, to world war, in the age of mass extermination.

III

Today, every inhabitant of this planet must contemplate the day when this planet may no longer be habitable. Every man, woman and child lives under a nuclear sword of Damocles, hanging by the slenderest of threads, capable of being cut at any moment by accident or miscalculation or by madness. The weapons of war must be abolished before they abolish us.

Men no longer debate whether armaments are a symptom or a cause of tension. The mere existence of modern weapons—ten million times more powerful than anything the world has ever seen, and only minutes away from any target on earth—is a source of horror, and discord and distrust. Men no longer maintain that disarmament must await the settlement of all disputes—for disarmament must be a part of any permanent settlement. And men may no longer pretend that the quest for disarmament is a sign of weakness—for in a spiraling arms race, a nation's security may well be shrinking even as its arms increase.

For fifteen years this organization has sought the reduction and destruction of arms. Now that goal is no longer a dream—it is a practical matter of life or death. The risks inherent in disarmament pale in comparison to the risks inherent in an unlimited arms race.

It is in this spirit that the recent Belgrade Conference—recognizing that this is no longer a Soviet problem or an American problem, but a human problem—endorsed a program of "general, complete and strictly an internationally controlled disarmament." It is in this same spirit that we in the United States have labored this year, with a new urgency, and with a new, now-statutory agency fully endorsed by the Congress, to find an approach to disarmament which would be so far-reaching yet realistic, so mutually balanced and beneficial, that it could be accepted by every nation. And it is in this spirit that we have presented with the agreement of the Soviet Union—under the label both nations now accept of "general and complete disarmament"—a new statement of newly-agreed principles for negotiation.

But we are well aware that all issues of principle are not settled—and that principles alone are not enough. It is therefore our intention to challenge the Soviet Union, not to an arms race, but to a peace race—to advance together step by step, stage by stage, until general and complete disarmament has been achieved. We invite them now to go beyond agreement in principle to reach agreement on actual plans.

The program to be presented to this Assembly—for general and complete disarmament under effective international control —moves to bridge the gap between those who insist on a gradual approach and those who talk only of the final and total achievement. It would create machinery to keep the peace as it destroys the machines of war. It would proceed through balanced and safeguarded stages designed to give no state a military advantage over another. It would place the final responsibility for verification and control where it belongs—not with the big powers alone, not with one's adversary or one's self—but in an international organization within the framework of the United Nations. It would assure that indispensable condition of disarmament—true inspection—and apply it in stages proportionate to the stage of disarmament. It would cover delivery systems as well as weapons. It would ultimately halt their production as well as their testing, their transfer as well as their possession. It would achieve, under the eye of an international disarmament organization, a steady reduction in forces, both nuclear and conventional, until it has abolished all armies and all weapons except those needed for internal order and a new United Nations Peace Force. And it starts that process now, today, even as the talks begin.

In short, general and complete disarmament must no longer be a slogan, used to resist the first steps. It is no longer to be a goal without means of achieving it, without means of verifying its progress, without means of keeping the peace. It is now a realistic plan, and a test—a test of those only willing to talk and a test of those willing to act.

Such a plan would not bring a world free from conflict or greed—but it would bring a world free from the terrors of mass destruction. It would not usher in the era of the super state— but it would usher in an era in which no state could annihilate or be annihilated by another.

In 1945, this nation proposed the Baruch Plan to internationalize the atom before other nations even possessed the bomb or demilitarized their troops. We proposed with our allies the disarmament plan of 1951 while still at war in Korea. And we make our proposals today, while building up our defenses over Berlin, not because we are inconsistent or insincere or intimidated, but because we know the rights of free men will prevail—because while we are compelled against our will to rearm, we look confidently beyond Berlin to the kind of disarmed world we all prefer.

I therefore propose, on the basis of this plan, that disarmament negotiations resume promptly, and continue without interruption until an entire program for general and complete disarmament has not only been agreed but has been actually achieved.

IV

The logical place to begin is a treaty assuring the end of nuclear tests of all kinds, in every environment, under workable controls. The United States and the United Kingdom have proposed such a treaty that is both reasonable, effective and ready for signature. We are still prepared to sign that treaty today.

We also proposed a mutual ban on atmospheric testing, without inspection or control, in order to save the human race from the poison of radioactive fall-out. We regret that that offer was not accepted.

For fifteen years we have sought to make the atom an instrument of peaceful growth rather than of war. But for fifteen years our concessions have been matched by obstruction, our patience by intransigence. And the pleas of mankind for peace have met with disregard.

Finally, as the explosions of others beclouded the skies, my country was left with no alternative but to act in the interests of its own and the free world's security. We cannot endanger that security by refraining from testing while others improve their arsenals. Nor can we endanger it by another long, unin-spected ban on testing. For three years we accepted those risks in our open society while seeking agreement on inspection. But this year, while we were negotiating in good faith in Geneva, others were secretly preparing new experiments in destruction.

Our tests are not polluting the atmosphere. Our deterrent weapons are guarded against accidental explosion or use. Our doctors and scientists stand ready to help any nation measure and meet the hazards to health which inevitably result from the tests in the atmosphere.

But to halt the spread of these terrible weapons, to halt the contamination of the air, to halt the spiraling nuclear arms race, we remain ready to seek new avenues of agreement, our new disarmament program thus includes the following proposals:

First, signing the test-ban treaty by all nations. This can be done now. Test-ban negotiations need not and should not await general disarmament.

Second, stopping the production of fissionable materials for use in weapons, and preventing their transfer to any nation now lacking in nuclear weapons.

Third, prohibiting the transfer of control over nuclear weapons to states that do not own them.

Fourth, keeping nuclear weapons from seeding new battle-grounds in outer space.

Fifth, gradually destroying existing nuclear weapons and converting their materials to peaceful uses; and

Finally, halting the unlimited testing and production of strategic nuclear delivery vehicles, and gradually destroying them as well.

V

To destroy arms, however, is not enough. We must create even as we destroy—creating world-wide law and law enforce-ment as we outlaw world-wide war and weapons. In the world we seek, the United Nations Emergency Forces which have been hastily assembled, uncertainly supplied and inadequately financed will never be enough.

Therefore, the United States recommends that all member nations earmark special peace-keeping units in their armed forces—to be on call of the United Nations—to be specially trained and quickly available—and with advance provision for financial and logistic support.

In addition, the American delegation will suggest a series of steps to improve the United Nations' machinery for the peaceful settlement of disputes—for on-the-spot fact-finding, mediation and adjudication—for extending the rule of international law. For peace is not solely a matter of military or technical problems —it is primarily a problem of politics and people. And unless man can match his strides in weaponry and technology with equal strides in social and political development, our great strength, like that of the dinosaur, will become incapable of proper control —and like the dinosaur vanish from the earth.

VI

As we extend the rule of law on earth, so must we also extend it to man's new domain: outer space.

All of us salute the brave cosmonauts of the Soviet Union. The new horizons of outer space must not be driven by the old bitter concepts of imperialism and sovereign claims. The cold reaches of the universe must not become the new arena of an even colder war.

To this end, we shall urge proposals extending the United Nations Charter to the limits of man's exploration in the universe, reserving outer space for peaceful use, prohibiting weapons of mass destruction in space or on celestial bodies, and opening the mysteries and benefits of space to every nation. We shall further propose cooperative efforts between all nations in weather prediction and eventually in weather control. We shall propose, finally, a global system of communications satellites linking the whole world in telegraph and telephone and radio and television. The day need not be far away when such a system will televise the proceedings of this body to every corner of the world for the benefit of peace.

VII

But the mysteries of outer space must not divert our eyes or our energies from the harsh realities that face our fellow men.

Political sovereignty is but a mockery without the means of meeting poverty and illiteracy and disease. Self-determination is but a slogan if the future holds no hope.

That is why my nation—which has freely shared its capital and its technology to help others help themselves—now proposes officially designating this decade of the 1960's as the United Nations Decade of Development. Under the framework of that resolution, the United Nations' existing efforts in promoting economic growth can be expanded and coordinated. Regional surveys and training institutes can now pool the talents of many. New research, technical assistance and pilot projects can unlock the wealth of less developed lands and untapped waters. And development can become a cooperative and not a competitive enterprise—to enable all nations, however diverse in their systems and beliefs, to become in fact as well as in law free and equal nations.

VIII

My country favors a world of free and equal states. We agree with those who say that colonialism is a key issue in this Assembly. But let the full facts of that issue be discussed in full.

On the one hand is the fact that, since the close of World War II, a world-wide declaration of independence has transformed nearly 1 billion people and 9 million square miles into 42 free and independent states. Less than 2 per cent of the world's population now lives in "dependent" territories.

I do not ignore the remaining problems of traditional colonialism which still confront this body. Those problems will be solved, with patience, good will and determination. Within the limits of our responsibility in such matters, my country intends to be a participant and not merely an observer, in the peaceful, expeditious movement of nations from the status of colonies to the partnership of equals. That continuing tide of self-determination, which runs so strong, has our sympathy and our support.

But colonialism in its harshest forms is not only the exploitation of new nations by old, of dark skins by light—or the subjugation of the poor by the rich. My nation was once a colony—and we know what colonialism means; the exploitation and subjugation of the weak by the powerful, of the many by the few, of the governed who have given no consent to be governed, whatever their continent, their class or their color.

And that is why there is no ignoring the fact that the tide of self-determination has not reached the Communist empire where a population far larger than that officially termed "dependent" lives under governments installed by foreign troops instead of free institutions—under a system which knows only one party and one belief—which suppresses free debate, and free elections, and free newspapers, and free books and free trade unions—and which builds a wall to keep truth a stranger and its own citizens prisoners. Let us debate colonialism in full—and apply the principle of free choice and the practice of free plebiscites in every corner of the globe.

IX

Finally, as President of the United States, I consider it my duty to report to this Assembly on two threats to the peace which are not on your crowded agenda, but which cause us, and most of you, the deepest concern.

The first threat on which I wish to report is widely misunderstood: the smoldering coals of war in southeast Asia. South Vietnam is already under attack—sometimes by a single assassin, sometimes by a band of guerrillas, recently by full battalions. The peaceful borders of Burma, Cambodia and India have been repeatedly violated. And the peaceful people of Laos are in danger of losing the independence they gained not so long ago.

No one can call these "wars of liberation." For these are free countries living under governments. Nor are these aggressions any less real because men are knifed in their homes and not shot in the fields of battle.

The very simple question confronting the world community is whether measures can be devised to protect the small and weak from such tactics. For if they are successful in Laos and South Vietnam, the gates will be opened wide.

The United States seeks for itself no base, no territory, no special position in this area of any kind. We support a truly neutral and independent Laos, its people free from outside interference, living at peace with themselves and with their neighbors, assured that their territory will not be used for attacks on others, and under a government comparable (as Mr. Khrushchev and I agreed at Vienna) to Cambodia and Burma.

But now the negotiations over Laos are reaching a crucial stage. The cease-fire is at best precarious. The rainy season is coming to an end. Laotian territory is being used to infiltrate South Vietnam. The world community must recognize—all those who are involved—that this potent threat to Laotian peace and freedom is indivisible from all other threats to their own.

Secondly, I wish to report to you on the crisis over Germany and Berlin. This is not the time or the place for immoderate tones, but the world community is entitled to know the very simple issues as we see them. If there is a crisis it is because an existing peace is under threat—because an existing island of free people is under pressure—because solemn agreements are being treated with indifference. Established international rights are being threatened with unilateral usurpation. Peaceful circulation has been interrupted by barbed wire and concrete blocks.

One recalls the order of the Czar in Pushkin's *Boris Godunov*: "Take steps at this very hour that our frontiers be fenced in by barriers. . . . That not a single soul pass o'er the border, that not a hare be able to run or a crow to fly."

It is absurd to allege that we are threatening a war merely to prevent the Soviet Union and East Germany from signing a so-called "treaty" of peace. The Western Allies are not concerned with any paper arrangement the Soviets may wish to make with a regime of their own creation, on territory occupied by their own troops and governed by their own agents. No such action can affect either our rights or our responsibilities.

If there is a dangerous crisis in Berlin—and there is—it is because of threats against the vital interests and the deep commitments of the Western powers, and the freedom of West Berlin. We cannot yield these interests. We cannot fail these commitments. We cannot surrender the freedom of these people for whom we are responsible. A "peace treaty" which carried with it the provisions which destroy the peace would be a fraud.

A "free city" which was not genuinely free would suffocate freedom and would be an infamy.

For a city or a people to be truly free, they must have the secure right, without economic, political or police pressure, to make their own choice and to live their own lives. And as I have said before, if anyone doubts the extent to which our presence is desired by the people of West Berlin, we are ready to have that question submitted to a free vote in all Berlin and, if possible, among all the German people.

The elementary fact about this crisis is that it is unnecessary. The elementary tools for a peaceful settlement are to be found in the Charter. Under its law, agreements are to be kept, unless changed by all those who made them. Established rights are to be respected. The political disposition of peoples should rest upon their own wishes, freely expressed in plebiscites or free elections. If there are legal problems, they can be solved by legal means. If there is a threat of force, it must be rejected. If there is desire for change, it must be a subject for negotiation and if there is negotiation, it must be rooted in mutual respect and concern for the rights of others.

The Western powers have calmly resolved to defend, by whatever means are forced upon them, their obligations and their access to the free citizens of West Berlin and the self-determination of those citizens. This generation learned from bitter experience that either brandishing or yielding to threats can only lead to war. But firmness and reason can lead to the kind of peaceful solution in which my country profoundly believes.

We are committed to no rigid formula. We see no perfect solution. We recognize that troops and tanks can, for a time, keep a nation divided against its will, however unwise that policy may seem to us. But we believe a peaceful agreement is possible which protects the freedom of West Berlin and allied presence and access, while recognizing the historic and legitimate interests of others in assuring European security.

The possibilities of negotiation are now being explored; it is too early to report what the prospects may be. For our part, we would be glad to report at the appropriate time that a solution has been found. For there is no need for a crisis over Berlin, threatening the peace—and if those who created this crisis desire peace, there will be peace and freedom in Berlin.

X

The events and decisions of the next ten months may well decide the fate of man for the next ten thousand years. There will be no avoiding those events. There will be no appeal from these decisions. And we in this hall shall be remembered either as part of the generation that turned this planet into a flaming funeral pyre or the generation that met its vow "to save succeeding generations from the scourge of war."

In the endeavor to meet that vow, I pledge you every effort this nation possesses. I pledge you that we shall neither commit nor provoke aggression—that we shall neither flee nor invoke the threat of force—that we shall never negotiate out of fear, we shall never fear to negotiate.

Terror is not a new weapon. Throughout history it has been used by those who could not prevail, either by persuasion or example. But inevitably they fail—either because men are not afraid to die for a life worth living—or because the terrorists themselves came to realize that free men can not be frightened by threats, and that aggression would meet its own response. And it is in the light of that history that every nation today should know, be he friend or foe, that the United States has both the will and the weapons to join free men in standing up to their responsibilities.

But I come here today to look across this world of threats to the world of peace. In that search we cannot expect any final triumph—for new problems will always arise. We cannot expect that all nations will adopt like systems—for conformity is the jailor of freedom, and the enemy of growth. Nor can we expect to reach our goal by contrivance, by fiat or even by the wishes of all.

But however close we sometimes seem to that dark and final abyss, let no man of peace and freedom depair. For he does not stand alone. If we all can persevere—if we can in every land and office look beyond our own shores and ambitions—then surely the age will dawn in which the strong are just and the weak secure and the peace preserved.

Ladies and gentlemen of this Assembly—the decision is ours. Never have the nations of the world had so much to lose—or so much to gain. Together we shall save our planet—or together we shall perish in its flames. Save it we can—and save it we must—and then shall we earn the eternal thanks of mankind and, as peacemakers, the eternal blessing of God.

THE UNITED STATES IN THE UNITED NATIONS: AN INDEPENDENT AUDIT [9]

HENRY M. JACKSON [10]

Arguments about its role and value began on the day the United Nations came into existence. They have never let up. The United States is clearly committed to the organization, and is intent upon preserving its integrity. But there can be no doubt that persuasion must continually be used to keep certain sections of the public well-disposed toward this international body. It was not for idle reason that a heading in a recent issue of the *Congressional Record* read: "Is the United Nations worth saving?" The speaker thought so, but he knew that he was dealing with an arguable question.

The latest controversy grew largely out of the UN action in the Congo. Initiated in 1960, the effort to enforce the peace ran into financial difficulties because the Soviet bloc and many Arab nations refused to support the undertaking. Added to the continuing costs of UN supervision of the Israeli-Egyptian border, the deficits soon became staggering. In order to meet the emergency, President Kennedy requested authority from Congress to subscribe to half of the $200 million issue of United Nations bonds.

The current debates, however, go beyond the question of the UN's ability to enforce the peace. Critics are asking whether the interests of the free world can be served more effectively through closer union in an Atlantic Community. And leaders in both political parties speculate whether our national policy is being unduly influenced by the force of "world opinion" as expressed through the General Assembly of the United Nations. These are the central inquiries raised by Senator Henry M. Jackson (Democrat, Washington) in his speech before the National Press Club in Washington, D.C., on March 20, 1962.

Senator Jackson did not condemn the United Nations. In fact, he was doubly cautious in disavowing such intent. In a carefully worded speech, he merely asked a few critical questions, three of which made up the summary of his talk:

> Do our present relations with the United Nations assist the wise definition of our vital interests and the establishment of sound policies? Are we sometimes deferring to the United Nations in the hope that we may somehow escape the in-

---

[9] Text furnished by Senator Jackson, with permission for this reprint.
[10] For biographical note, see Appendix.

escapable dilemmas of leadership? Are we failing to make the most of the United Nations by encouraging it to attempt too much?

With tact and prudence, Senator Jackson explored the doubts suggested by his own questions. The implications of his answers were clear. Reporting in the New York *Herald Tribune,* Marguerite Higgins viewed the speech as "the only carefully considered critique of the Kennedy Administration's foreign policy made in recent days by a respected Democratic liberal, as distinguished, for example, from the Republican National Committee, Republican leaders and, to the Far Right, the John Birchites."

Reaction to Senator Jackson's speech came swiftly. Speaking to several hundred press, radio, and television representatives in Washington on March 26, Under Secretary of State George W. Ball said there was "no contradiction between United States support of the United Nations and the Atlantic Community." "I find it a curious concept," he remarked, "that in world affairs we can do only one thing at a time." Writing in the New York *Times Magazine* on April 1, Harlan Cleveland, Assistant Secretary of State for International Organization Affairs, expressed a similar view: "In playing on the great organ of international relations, it is not enough to stomp on the pedal of unilateral action, or pick out a thin melody on one of the several international consoles before us. . . . We are big boys now, and we have learned how to do more than one thing at a time in our foreign policy."

The place of the United Nations in American foreign policy is now receiving a good deal of attention. Unfortunately, the debate seems to be polarized around extreme positions. On the one hand, there are those who say, "The UN is the only source of hope, let's leave everything to the UN." On the other hand, there are those who say, "The UN is the source of catastrophe, let's get out of the UN." Each view is like the distorted reflection in a carnival mirror—one too broad, the other too narrow. Neither view is really helpful.

No doubt the quiet, steadying majority of the American people have a more balanced view of the United Nations, and see it for what it is: an aspiration and a hope, the closest approximation we have to a code of international good conduct, and a useful forum of diplomacy for some purposes.

The United Nations is, and should continue to be, an important avenue of American foreign policy. Yet practices have developed which, I believe, lead to an undue influence of UN considerations in our national decision making. Indeed it is necessary to ask whether the involvement of the UN in our policy making has not at times hampered the wise definition of our national interests and the development of sound policies for their advancement.

The test of the national security policy process is this: Does it identify our vital interests and does it develop foreign and defense policies which will defend and promote these interests? In our system, two men must bear the heaviest responsibility for giving our national security policy focus and structure. One is, of course, the President. The other is his first adviser, the Secretary of State.

The United Nations is not, and was never intended to be, a substitute for our own leaders as makers and movers of American policy. The shoulders of the Secretary-General were never expected to carry the burdens of the President or the Secretary of State. But do we sometimes act as though we could somehow subcontract to the UN the responsibility for national decision making?

At the founding of the United Nations there was the hope that all its members shared a common purpose—the search for a lasting peace. This hope was dashed.

The Soviet Union was not and is not a "peace-loving" nation. Khrushchev has announced his support for "wars of liberation." He has threatened to "bury" us. In their more agreeable moments the Russians promise to bury us nicely, but whatever their mood, the earth would still be six feet deep above us.

We must realize that the Soviet Union sees the UN not as a forum of cooperation, but as one more arena of struggle.

The maintenance of peace depends not on the United Nations as an organization but on the strength and will of its members to uphold the Charter.

The truth is, though we have not often spoken it in recent years, that the best hope for peace with justice does not lie in the United Nations. Indeed, the truth is almost exactly the reverse. The best hope for the United Nations lies in the maintenance of peace. In our deeply divided world, peace depends on the power and unity of the Atlantic Community and on the skill of our direct diplomacy.

In this light, some basic questions need to be asked:

First: Are we taking an exaggerated view of the UN's role?

In one way and another the conduct of UN affairs absorbs a disproportionate amount of the energy of our highest officials. The President and the Secretary of State must ration their worry time—and the hours spent on the UN cannot be spent on other matters. All too often, furthermore, the energies devoted to the UN must be spent on defensive actions—trying to defeat this or that ill-advised resolution—rather than on more constructive programs.

The Secretary of State has called the United Nations "a forum in which almost every aspect of our foreign policy comes up." The fact is correctly stated, but does it reflect a desirable state of affairs? Should we take a more restricted view of the organization's capacity for helpfulness?

I think we should. The cold war may destroy the United Nations, if that organization becomes one of its main battle-grounds, but the United Nations cannot put an end to the cold war.

As a general rule, might it be more prudent, though less dramatic, not to push the UN into the fireman's suit unless we are sure the alternatives are worse and, above all, that we are not seeking to evade our own responsibilities.

I believe the United Nations can best gain stature and respect by undertaking tasks which are within its capabilities, and that its usefulness will be diminished if it is impelled into one cold war crisis after another and asked to shoulder responsibilities it cannot meet.

With these thoughts in mind, I read with some concern proposals to increase the "executive responsibilities" of the organization. Also, I have serious doubts about current suggestions to provide "more pervasive and efficient 'UN presences'" to help "halt infiltration of guerrillas across frontiers; and to help halt internal subversion instigated by a foreign power...."

Dag Hammarskjold, who was a brilliant and devoted servant of the United Nations, clearly saw the dangers in overrating the peace-keeping power of the organization. In a letter to a private citizen, he once decried the tendency to force the Secretary-General into a key role in great power disputes "through sheer escapism from those who should carry the responsibility".

Second: May not the most useful function of the United Nations lie in serving as a link between the West and the newly independent states?

Most international business is best handled through normal bilateral contacts or through regional arrangements among the states concerned.

However, the United Nations provides a useful meeting ground for many new governments with other governments. These relationships may be of mutual benefit.

The UN affords good opportunities to explain Western policies, to correct misrepresentations of the Western position, and to expose the weaknesses in the Soviet line. In fact, the Soviet singing commercials themselves offend the most hardened ear. They inspire a healthy skepticism about Russian three-way cold war pills—guaranteed to end the arms race, relieve colonial oppression, and ease poverty, if taken regularly, as directed.

The UN and its specialized agencies may be of great usefulness in supplying technical assistance for economic development, in providing financial aid, and in preparing international development programs.

The organization may sometimes be helpful in reaching peaceful settlements of certain issues and disputes of concern to the newly independent states—especially if it is used to seek out areas of agreement rather than to dramatize conflicts of interest.

In this connection there has been too great a tendency to bring every issue to a vote. Indeed, there are too many votes on too many issues in the UN—and too much of the time and energy of every delegation is spent in lobbying for votes.

A vote requires a division of the house, a sharpening and even an exaggeration of points at issue, and it emphasizes the division of opinion rather than the area of agreement. Not every discussion needs to end in a vote. The purposes of the members might be better served if the UN forum becomes more often a place where diplomatic representatives quietly search for acceptable settlements of issues between their countries.

Voting has a way of raising the temperatures of any body, and I think that we should be doing what we can to keep the temperature of the United Nations near normal.

Third: In our approach to the UN, do we make too much of the talk and too little of the deed?

New York City is the foremost communications center of the United States, if not of the world. Once the decision was made to locate the headquarters of the United Nations in New York, it was inevitable that what went on there would receive attention disproportionate to its significance. Newsmen and photographers have to produce news stories and pictures, and politicians from any land rival the celebrities of stage and screen in their hunger for free publicity.

The United States is of course host to the United Nations. Day in and day out we are conscious of the presence of the organization in our midst. And the role of host entails special obligations. Consequently, it is often difficult to keep one's sense of proportion. There is, for example, a tendency, to which the press itself is not immune, to believe the UN makes more history than it really does.

A Secretary of State—responsible for policy—must weigh his words carefully. For that reason he seldom makes good copy. One of the reasons for the extensive coverage of the United Nations is that the right to the floor of the General Assembly is not subject to the sobering influence of responsibilities for action.

I have been struck, for example, by the serious disproportion in the press, radio, and television coverage of our UN delegation and the coverage of the Department of State. The space and time devoted to the former does not correctly reflect the relative importance of what is said in New York against what is said in Washington.

If the UN were used less for drumbeating on every nerve-tingling issue, and if its energies were quietly devoted to manageable problems, there might be fewer headlines from the UN but more contributions to the building of a peaceful world.

Everyone talks too much. It is a world-wide disease. Sometimes it seems that the appropriate legend to place above the portals of the UN might be: "Through these doors pass the most articulate men and women in the world."

Fourth: Should our delegation to the United Nations play a larger role in the policy-making process than our representatives to NATO or to major world capitals?

I think the answer is no, and the burden of proof should lie with those who advocate a unique role for our embassy in New York.

Our delegation to the United Nations is, of course, frequently and necessarily involved in promoting or opposing particular actions by the United Nations which may have an important bearing on our national security policies. If it is not to commit the United States to positions inconsistent with our national security requirements, the delegation must be kept in closest touch with, and have a thorough understanding of, these requirements. Furthermore, the President and Secretary of State require information and advice from our UN delegation.

This is not to say, however, that the requirements of sound national policy can be more clearly seen in New York than elsewhere, or that our embassy in New York should play a different role in policy-making from that played by other important embassies.

The precedent set by President Eisenhower in this matter, and continued by this Administration, seems unfortunate. The Ambassador to the United Nations is not a second Secretary of State, but the present arrangement suggests a certain imbalance in the role assigned to the UN delegation in the policy-making process.

The problem is not to give the UN delegation a larger voice in policy-making but to give it the tools to help carry out the policy.

Rational, effective negotiation on complex and critical matters, like the reduction and control of armaments, requires unified guidance and instruction to those conducting the negotiations. This is a basic principle of sound administration and avoids the dangers of freewheeling. The unified source of instructions should be the Secretary of State, acting for the President, or the President himself—not others in the White House or the Executive Office, not lower levels in State, certainly not the UN delegation itself.

The UN delegation in New York should not operate as a second foreign office. Such confusion of responsibility reinforces a tendency to give undue weight in national policy formulation to considerations that seem more important in New York than they ought to seem in Washington, D.C. The effect of decisions on something called "our relations in the UN" may receive more weight than their effect on, say, the strength and unity of the Atlantic Community. The result may be a weakening or dilution of policy positions in deference to what is represented in New York as world opinion.

The concept of world opinion has been, I fear, much abused. Whatever it is and whatever the importance that should be attached to it, I doubt that it can be measured by taking the temperature of the General Assembly or successfully cultivated primarily by currying favor in New York. To hide behind something called "world opinion" is all too often the device of the timid, or the last resort of someone who has run out of arguments.

Fifth: Is our UN delegation properly manned for the diplomatic and technical tasks we require of it?

We have established the tradition of choosing for top UN posts Americans of considerable prestige—prestige acquired, furthermore, not in the practice of diplomacy but in national politics, business, the arts and sciences and other fields of endeavor. For the most part, these people have served us well, in effective advocacy of America's concerns, and in persuasive championship of progress toward a world of good neighbors.

A start has been made in staffing the UN mission more as other embassies, with experienced diplomats and experts in technical fields in which the United Nations may be able to make quiet but useful contributions. Further progress in this direction should be encouraged.

The sum of the matter is this:

We need to take another look at our role in the United Nations, remembering that the UN is not a substitute for national policies wisely conceived to uphold our vital interests. We need to rethink the organization and staffing of our government for United Nations affairs.

For this purpose, we should have a top-level review conducted under the authority of the President and the Secretary of State. The review should, of course, be handled in a nonpartisan manner.

Debate over the United Nations is now centered on the UN bond issue. This debate reveals some of the symptoms of the basic disturbance. Congress has been requested to approve the purchase of UN bonds up to a total of $100 million to help cover the cost of two controversial peace-keeping operations. The money in question has been spent and it would be a serious mistake to prolong the financial crisis. I trust the Congress can help find a wise way to help cover the deficit.

But the fundamental questions will still remain, and will plague us until they are answered:

Do our present relations with the United Nations assist the wise definition of our vital interests and the establishment of sound policies? Are we sometimes deferring to the United Nations in the hope that we may somehow escape the inescapable dilemmas of leadership? Are we failing to make the most of the United Nations by encouraging it to attempt too much?

Mr. Chairman, I close as I began: The United Nations is, and should continue to be, an important avenue of American foreign policy. But we need to revise our attitudes in the direction of a more realistic appreciation of its limitations, more modest hopes for its accomplishments, and a more mature sense of the burdens of responsible leadership.

SOME VIEWS ON WHAT CONSTITUTES
THE PUBLIC INTEREST

TELEVISION AND THE PUBLIC INTEREST [1]

NEWTON N. MINOW [2]

Newton N. Minow, chairman of the Federal Communications Commission, started a lively discussion in 1961. And it is still going on. According to John Crosby, former television critic of the New York *Herald Tribune,* Mr. Minow committed an unpardonable act for a man in his position: he watched television. Evidently what he saw did not please him completely.

So on May 9, 1961, in Washington, D.C., he addressed some two thousand persons attending the thirty-ninth annual convention of the National Association of Broadcasters. What he said has furnished copy for continuing controversy among critics, politicians, advertising men, and broadcasters—indeed, among many of the 180 million informed Americans who gather around the 56 million sets reportedly in use.

Describing a considerable part of television programing as "a vast wasteland," Mr. Minow spelled out what he thought was wrong, what the broadcasters' obligations were, and what should be done to improve the medium and restore public confidence in it. Much of what he said had of course been said before, as he freely acknowledged. LeRoy Collins, in an address reprinted in last year's REPRESENTATIVE AMERICAN SPEECHES, candidly assessed television's alleged faults when he assumed the presidency of the National Association of Broadcasters. Moreover, in his keynote address to the NAB convention on May 8, 1961, Mr. Collins spoke at length about the need for more diversity and quality in programing. He also said that television's full potential could never be realized until broadcasters started *taking sides,* started editorializing on public issues. "You must help Americans and others to understand better this complex, rapidly-changing world and show them how they can become more significant parts of its movement." In an address before the NAB in Washington, D.C., on March 1, 1962, Mr. Minow declared that if it is "to take its rightful place in the communications firmament . . . broadcasting should be willing to express a point of view about the news it provides."

[1] Text furnished by Tedson J. Meyers, administrative assistant to Mr. Minow, with permission for this reprint.

[2] For biographical note, see Appendix.

The apparent similarity of views held by Mr. Minow and Mr. Collins led, in the opinion of Jack Gould, radio and television critic of the New York *Times,* to an ironic consequence. Because certain broadcasters felt that it would be "rather awkward . . . to disagree with the man they picked as their spokesman," Mr. Collins' initiative had the effect of shutting off "the flow of dissent." By early fall of 1961, however, this comment had lost its force, as the introduction to Dr. Frank Stanton's speech, also included in this section, will indicate.

Mr. Minow's talk carried unusual impact. It was a voice from official Washington. It pointed out that television had great influence, and that it made a difference whether the programs aimed at high or low targets.

The speech aroused strong expectation for improvement in programing, as well as deep concern over possible governmental intervention. The Federal Communications Commission passes upon license renewals every three years. Some broadcasters feared that the licensing power might be used as a club to promote the Commission's notion of good television. At any rate, Mr. Minow's speech brought into focus what Jack Gould considered "the fundamental differences of philosophy concerning the relationship between government and industry in a field that deals with the volatile commodities of ideas and tastes."

Thank you for this opportunity to meet with you today. This is my first public address since I took over my new job. When the New Frontiersmen rode into town, I locked myself in my office to do my homework and get my feet wet. But apparently I haven't managed to stay out of hot water. I seem to have detected a certain nervous apprehension about what I might say or do when I emerged from that locked office for this, my maiden station break.

First, let me begin by dispelling a rumor. I was not picked for this job because I regard myself as the fastest draw on the New Frontier.

Second, let me start a rumor. Like you, I have carefully read President Kennedy's messages about the regulatory agencies, conflict of interest, and the dangers of *ex parte* contacts. And of course, we at the Federal Communications Commission will do our part. Indeed, I may even suggest that we change the name of the FCC to The Seven Untouchables!

It may also come as a surprise to some of you, but I want you to know that you have my admiration and respect. Yours is a most honorable profession. Anyone who is in the broadcasting business has a tough row to hoe. You earn your bread by using public property. When you work in broadcasting you volunteer for public service, public pressure, and public regulation. You must compete with other attractions and other investments, and the only way you can do it is to prove to us every three years that you should have been in business in the first place.

I can think of easier ways to make a living.

But I cannot think of more satisfying ways.

I admire your courage—but that doesn't mean I would make life any easier for you. Your license lets you use the public's airwaves as trustees for 180 million Americans. The public is your beneficiary. If you want to stay on as trustees, you must deliver a decent return to the public—not only to your stockholders. So, as a representative of the public, your health and your product are among my chief concerns.

As to your health: let's talk only of television today. Nineteen sixty gross broadcast revenues of the television industry were over $1,268,000,000; profit before taxes was $243,900,000, an average return on revenue of 19.2 per cent. Compared with 1959, gross broadcast revenues were $1,163,900,000, and profit before taxes was $222,300,000, an average return on revenue of 19.1 per cent. So, the percentage increase of total revenues from 1959 to 1960 was 9 per cent, and the percentage increase of profit was 9.7 per cent. This, despite a recession. For your investors, the price has indeed been right.

I have confidence in your health.

But not in your product.

It is with this and much more in mind that I come before you today.

One editorialist in the trade press wrote that "the FCC of the New Frontier is going to be one of the toughest FCC's in the history of broadcast regulation." If he meant that we intend to enforce the law in the public interest, let me make it perfectly clear that he is right—we do.

If he meant that we intend to muzzle or censor broadcasting, he is dead wrong.

It would not surprise me if some of you had expected me to come here today and say in effect, "Clean up your own house or the government will do it for you."

Well, in a limited sense, you would be right—I've just said it.

But I want to say to you earnestly that it is not in that spirit that I come before you today, nor is it in that spirit that I intend to serve the FCC.

I am in Washington to help broadcasting, not to harm it; to strengthen it, not weaken it; to reward it, not punish it; to encourage it, not threaten it; to stimulate it, not censor it.

Above all, I am here to uphold and protect the public interest.

What do we mean by "the public interest?" Some say the public interest is merely what interests the public.

I disagree.

So does your distinguished president, Governor Collins. In a recent speech he said,

> Broadcasting to serve the public interest, must have a soul and a conscience, a burning desire to excel, as well as to sell; the urge to build the character, citizenship and intellectual stature of people, as well as to expand the gross national product. . . . By no means do I imply that broadcasters disregard the public interest. . . . But a much better job can be done, and should be done.

I could not agree more.

And I would add that in today's world, with chaos in Laos and the Congo aflame, with Communist tyranny on our Caribbean doorstep and relentless pressure on our Atlantic alliance, with social and economic problems at home of the gravest nature, yes, and with technological knowledge that makes it possible, as our President has said, not only to destroy our world but to destroy poverty around the world—in a time of peril and opportunity, the old complacent, unbalanced fare of action-adventure and situation comedies is simply not good enough.

Your industry possesses the most powerful voice in America. It has an inescapable duty to make that voice ring with intelligence and with leadership. In a few years, this exciting industry has grown from a novelty to an instrument of overwhelming impact on the American people. It should be making ready for the kind of leadership that newspapers and magazines assumed years ago, to make our people aware of their world.

Ours has been called the jet age, the atomic age, the space age. It is also, I submit, the television age. And just as history will decide whether the leaders of today's world employed the atom to destroy the world or rebuild it for mankind's benefit, so will history decide whether today's broadcasters employed their powerful voice to enrich the people or debase them.

If I seem today to address myself chiefly to the problems of television, I don't want any of you radio broadcasters to think we've gone to sleep at your switch—we haven't. We still listen. But in recent years most of the controversies and cross-currents in broadcast programing have swirled around television. And so my subject today is the television industry and the public interest.

Like everybody, I wear more than one hat. I am the chairman of the FCC. I am also a television viewer and the husband and father of other television viewers. I have seen a great many television programs that seemed to me eminently worth while and I am not talking about the much bemoaned good old days of "Playhouse 90" and "Studio One."

I am talking about this past season. Some were wonderfully entertaining, such as "The Fabulous Fifties," "The Fred Astaire Show," and "The Bing Crosby Special"; some were dramatic and moving, such as Conrad's "Victory" and "Twilight Zone"; some were marvelously informative, such as "The Nation's Future," "CBS Reports," and "The Valiant Years." I could list many more —programs that I am sure everyone here felt enriched his own life and that of his family. When television is good, nothing— not the theater, not the magazines or newspapers—nothing is better.

But when television is bad, nothing is worse. I invite you to sit down in front of your television set when your station goes on the air and stay there without a book, magazine, newspaper, profit and loss sheet or rating book to distract you—and keep your eyes glued to that set until the station signs off. I can assure you that you will observe a vast wasteland.

You will see a procession of game shows, violence, audience participation shows, formula comedies about totally unbelievable families, blood and thunder, mayhem, violence, sadism, murder, western badmen, western good men, private eyes, gangsters, more violence, and cartoons. And, endlessly, commercials—many screaming, cajoling, and offending. And most of all, boredom. True, you will see a few things you will enjoy. But they will be very, very few. And if you think I exaggerate, try it.

Is there one person in this room who claims that broadcasting can't do better?

Well, a glance at next season's proposed programing can give us little heart. Of 73½ hours of prime evening time, the networks have tentatively scheduled 59 hours to categories of action-adventure, situation comedy, variety, quiz, and movies.

Is there one network president in this room who claims he can't do better?

Well, is there at least one network president who believes that the other networks can't do better?

Gentlemen, your trust accounting with your beneficiaries is overdue.

Never have so few owed so much to so many.

Why is so much of television so bad? I have heard many answers: demands of your advertisers; competition for ever higher ratings; the need always to attract a mass audience; the high cost of television programs; the insatiable appetite for programing material—these are some of them. Unquestionably, these are tough problems not susceptible to easy answers.

But I am not convinced that you have tried hard enough to solve them.

I do not accept the idea that the present over-all programing is aimed accurately at the public taste. The ratings tell us only that some people have their television sets turned on and of that number, so many are tuned to one channel and so many to another. They don't tell us what the public might watch if they were offered half a dozen additional choices. A rating, at best, is an indication of how many people saw what you gave them. Unfortunately, it does not reveal the depth of the penetration, or the intensity of reaction, and it never reveals what the acceptance would have been if what you gave them had been better—if all the forces of art and creativity and daring and imagination had been unleashed. I believe in the people's good sense and good taste, and I am not convinced that the people's taste is as low as some of you assume.

My concern with the rating services is not with their accuracy. Perhaps they are accurate. I really don't know. What, then, is wrong with the ratings? It's not been their accuracy—it's been their use.

Certainly, I hope you will agree that ratings should have little influence where children are concerned. The best estimates indicate that during the hours of 5 to 6 P.M. sixty per cent of your audience is composed of children under twelve. And most young children today, believe it or not, spend as much time watching television as they do in the schoolroom. I repeat—let that sink in—most young children today spend as much time watching television as they do in the schoolroom. It used to be said that there were three great influences on a child: home, school, and church. Today, there is a fourth great influence, and you ladies and gentlemen control it.

If parents, teachers, and ministers conducted their responsibilities by following the ratings, children would have a steady diet of ice cream, school holidays, and no Sunday school. What about your responsibilities? Is there no room on television to teach, to inform, to uplift, to stretch, to enlarge the capacities of our children? Is there no room for programs deepening their understanding of children in other lands? Is there no room for a children's news show explaining something about the world to them at their level of understanding? Is there no room for reading the great literature of the past, teaching them the great traditions of freedom? There are some fine children's shows, but they are drowned out in the massive doses of cartoons, violence, and more violence. Must these be your trademarks? Search your consciences and see if you cannot offer more to your young beneficiaries whose future you guide so many hours each and every day.

What about adult programing and ratings? You know, newspaper publishers take popularity ratings too. The answers are pretty clear: it is almost always the comics, followed by the advice to the lovelorn columns. But, ladies and gentlemen, the news is still on the front page of all newspapers, the editorials are not replaced by more comics, the newspapers have not become one long collection of advice to the lovelorn. Yet newspapers do not need a license from the government to be in business—they do not use public property. But in television—where your responsibilities as public trustees are so plain, the moment that the ratings indicate that westerns are popular there are new imitations of westerns on the air faster than the old coaxial cable could take us from Hollywood to New York. Broadcasting cannot continue to live by the numbers. Ratings ought to be the slave of the broadcaster, not his master. And you and I both know that the rating services themselves would agree.

Let me make clear that what I am talking about is balance. I believe that the public interest is made up of many interests. There are many people in this great country and you must serve all of us. You will get no argument from me if you say that, given a choice between a western and a symphony, more people will watch the western. I like westerns and private eyes too—but a steady diet for the whole country is obviously not in the public interest. We all know that people would more often prefer to be entertained than stimulated or informed. But your obligations are not satisfied if you look only to popularity as a test of what to broadcast. You are not only in show business; you are free to communicate ideas as well as relaxation. You must provide a wider range of choices, more diversity, more alternatives. It is not enough to cater to the nation's whims—you must also serve the nation's needs.

And I would add this—that if some of you persist in a relentless search for the highest rating and the lowest common denominator, you may very well lose your audience. Because, to paraphrase a great American who was recently my law partner, the people are wise, wiser than some of the broadcasters—and politicians—think.

As you may have gathered, I would like to see television improved. But how is this to be brought about? By voluntary action by the broadcasters themselves? By direct government intervention? Or how?

Let me address myself now to my role not as a viewer but as chairman of the FCC. I could not if I would, chart for you this afternoon in detail all of the actions I contemplate. Instead, I want to make clear some of the fundamental principles which guide me.

First: the people own the air. They own it as much in prime evening time as they do at six o'clock Sunday morning. For every hour that the people give you—you owe them something. I intend to see that your debt is paid with service.

Second: I think it would be foolish and wasteful for us to continue any worn-out wrangle over the problems of payola, rigged quiz shows, and other mistakes of the past. There are laws on the books which we will enforce. But there is no chip on my shoulder. We live together in perilous, uncertain times; we face together staggering problems; and we must not waste much time now by rehashing the clichés of past controversy. To quarrel over the past is to lose the future.

Third: I believe in the free enterprise system. I want to see broadcasting improved and I want you to do the job. I am proud to champion your cause. It is not rare for American businessmen to serve a public trust. Yours is a special trust because it is imposed by law.

Fourth: I will do all I can to help educational television. There are still not enough educational stations, and major centers of the country still lack usable educational channels. If there were a limited number of printing presses in this country, you may be sure that a fair proportion of them would be put to educational use. Educational television has an enormous contribution to make to the future, and I intend to give it a hand along the way. If there is not a nation-wide educational television system in this country, it will not be the fault of the FCC.

Fifth: I am unalterably opposed to governmental censorship. There will be no suppression of programing which does not meet with bureaucratic tastes. Censorship strikes at the tap root of our free society.

Sixth: I did not come to Washington to idly observe the squandering of the public's airwaves. The squandering of our airwaves is no less important than the lavish waste of any precious natural resource. I intend to take the job of chairman of the FCC very seriously. I believe in the gravity of my own particular sector of the New Frontier. There will be times perhaps when you will consider that I take myself or my job *too* seriously. Frankly, I don't care if you do. For I am convinced that either one takes this job seriously—or one can be seriously taken.

Now, how will these principles be applied? Clearly, at the heart of the FCC's authority lies its power to license, to renew or fail to renew, or to revoke a license. As you know, when your license comes up for renewal, your performance is compared with your promises. I understand that many people feel that in the past licenses were often renewed *pro forma*. I say to you now:

renewal will not be *pro forma* in the future. There is nothing permanent or sacred about a broadcast license.

But simply matching promises and performance is not enough. I intend to do more. I intend to find out whether the people care. I intend to find out whether the community which each broadcaster serves believes he has been serving the public interest. When a renewal is set down for hearing, I intend—wherever possible—to hold a well-advertised public hearing, right in the community you have promised to serve. I want the people who own the air and the homes that television enters to tell you and the FCC what's been going on. I want the people—if they are truly interested in the service you give them—to make notes, document cases, tell us the facts. For those few of you who really believe that the public interest is merely what interests the public—I hope that these hearings will arouse no little interest.

The FCC has a fine reserve of monitors—almost 180 million Americans gathered around 56 million sets. If you want those monitors to be your friends at court—it's up to you.

Some of you may say, "Yes, but I still do not know where the line is between a grant of a renewal and the hearing you just spoke of." My answer is: Why should you want to know how close you can come to the edge of the cliff? What the Commission asks of you is to make a conscientious, good-faith effort to serve the public interest. Every one of you serves a community in which the people would benefit by educational, religious, instructive or other public service programing. Every one of you serves an area which has local needs—as to local elections, controversial issues, local news, local talent. Make a serious, genuine effort to put on that programing. When you do, you will not be playing brinkmanship with the public interest.

What I've been saying applies to broadcast stations. Now a station break for the networks:

You know your importance in this great industry. Today, more than one half of all hours of television station programing comes from the networks; in prime time, this rises to more than three quarters of the available hours.

You know that the FCC has been studying network operations for some time. I intend to press this to a speedy conclusion with useful results. I can tell you right now, however, that I am deeply concerned with concentration of power in the hands of the networks. As a result, too many local stations have foregone any efforts at local programing, with little use of live talent and local service. Too many local stations operate with one hand on the network switch and the other on a projector loaded with old movies. We want the individual stations to be free to meet their legal responsibilities to serve their communities.

I join Governor Collins in his views so well expressed to the advertisers who use the public air. I urge the networks to join him and undertake a very special mission on behalf of this industry: you can tell your advertisers, "This is the high quality we are going to serve—take it or other poeple will. If you think you can find a better place to move automobiles, cigarettes and soap—go ahead and try."

Tell your sponsors to be less concerned with costs per thousand and more concerned with understanding per millions. And remind your stockholders that an investment in broadcasting is buying a share in public responsibility.

The networks can start this industry on the road to freedom from the dictatorship of numbers.

But there is more to the problem than network influences on stations or advertiser influences on networks. I know the problems networks face in trying to clear some of their best programs— the informational programs that exemplify public service. They are your finest hours—whether sustaining or commercial, whether regularly scheduled or special—these are the signs that broadcasting knows the way to leadership. They make the public's trust in you a wise choice.

They should be seen. As you know, we are readying for use new forms by which broadcast stations will report their programing to the Commission. You probably also know that special attention will be paid in these reports to public service programing. I believe that stations taking network service should also be required to report the extent of the local clearance of network public service programing, and when they fail to clear them, they should explain why. If it is to put on some outstanding local program, this is one reason. But, if it is simply to carry some old movies, that is an entirely different matter. The Commission should consider such clearance reports carefully when making up its mind about the licensee's over-all programing.

We intend to move—and as you know, indeed the FCC was rapidly moving in other new areas before the new Administration arrived in Washington. And I want to pay my public respects to my very able predecessor, Fred Ford, and my colleagues on the Commission who have welcomed me to the FCC with warmth and cooperation.

We have approved an experiment with pay TV, and in New York we are testing the potential of UHF broadcasting. Either or both of these may revolutionize television. Only a foolish prophet would venture to guess the direction they will take, and their effect. But we intend that they shall be explored fully— for they are part of broadcasting's New Frontier.

The questions surrounding pay TV are largely economic. The questions surrounding UHF are largely technological. We are going to give the infant pay TV a chance to prove whether it can offer a useful service; we are going to protect it from those who would strangle it in its crib.

As for UHF, I'm sure you know about our test in the canyons of New York City. We will take every possible positive step to break through the allocations barrier into UHF. We will put this sleeping giant to use and in the years ahead we may have twice as many channels operating in cities where now there are only two or three. We may have a half dozen networks instead of three.

I have told you that I believe in the free enterprise system. I believe that most of television's problems stem from lack of competition. This is the importance of UHF to me: with more channels on the air, we will be able to provide every community with enough stations to offer service to all parts of the public. Programs with a mass market appeal required by mass product advertisers certainly will still be available. But other stations will recognize the need to appeal to more limited markets and to special tastes. In this way, we can all have a much wider range of programs.

Television should thrive on this competition—and the country should benefit from alternative sources of service to the public. And—Governor Collins—I hope the NAB will benefit from many new members.

Another and perhaps the most important frontier: television will rapidly join the parade into space. International television will be with us soon. No one knows how long it will be until a broadcast from a studio in New York will be viewed in India as well as in Indiana, will be seen in the Congo as it is seen in Chicago. But as surely as we are meeting here today, that day will come—and once again our world will shrink.

What will the people of other countries think of us when they see our western badmen and good men punching each other in the jaw in between the shooting? What will the Latin American or African child learn of America from our great communications industry? We cannot permit television in its present form to be our voice overseas.

There is your challenge to leadership. You must reexamine some fundamentals of your industry. You must open your minds and open your hearts to the limitless horizons of tomorrow.

I can suggest some words that should serve to guide you:

Television and all who participate in it are jointly accountable to the American public for respect for the special needs of children, for community responsibility, for the advancement of education and culture, for the acceptability of the program materials chosen, for decency and decorum in production, and for propriety in advertising. This responsibility cannot be discharged by any given group of programs, but can be discharged only through the highest standards of respect for the American home, applied to every moment of every program presented by television.

Program materials should enlarge the horizons of the viewer, provide him with wholesome entertainment, afford helpful stimulation, and remind him of the responsibilities which the citizen has towards his society.

These words are not mine. They are yours. They are taken literally from your own Television Code. They reflect the leadership and aspirations of your own great industry. I urge you to respect them as I do. And I urge you to respect the intelligent and farsighted leadership of Governor LeRoy Collins, and to make this meeting a creative act. I urge you at this meeting and, after you leave, back home, at your stations and your networks, to strive ceaselessly to improve your product and to better serve your viewers, the American people.

I hope that we at the FCC will not allow ourselves to become so bogged down in the mountain of papers, hearings, memoranda, orders, and the daily routine that we close our eyes to the wider view of the public interest. And I hope that you broadcasters will not permit yourselves to become so absorbed in the chase for ratings, sales, and profits that you lose this wider view. Now more than ever before in broadcasting's history the times demand the best of all of us.

We need imagination in programing, not sterility; creativity, not imitation; experimentation, not conformity; excellence, not mediocrity. Television is filled with creative, imaginative people. You must strive to set them free.

Television in its young life has had many hours of greatness— its "Victory at Sea," its Army-McCarthy hearings, its "Peter Pan," its "Kraft Theaters," its "See It Now," its "Project 20," the World Series, its political conventions and campaigns, the Great Debates—and it has had its endless hours of mediocrity and its moments of public disgrace. There are estimates that today the average viewer spends about 200 minutes daily with television, while the average reader spends 38 minutes with magazines and 40 minutes with newspapers. Television has grown faster than a teen-ager, and now it is time to grow up.

What you gentlemen broadcast through the people's air affects the people's taste, their knowledge, their opinions, their understanding of themselves and of their world. And their future.

The power of instantaneous sight and sound is without precedent in mankind's history. This is an awesome power. It has limitless capabilities for good—and for evil. And it carries with it awesome responsibilities, responsibilities which you and I cannot escape.

In his stirring inaugural address our President said, "And so, my fellow Americans: ask not what your country can do for you— ask what you can do for your country."

Ladies and Gentlemen:

Ask not what broadcasting can do for you. Ask what you can do for broadcasting.

I urge you to put the people's airwaves to the service of the people and the cause of freedom. You must help prepare a generation for great decisions. You must help a great nation fulfill its future.

Do this, and I pledge you our help.

BENJAMIN FRANKLIN LECTURE [3]

Frank Stanton [4]

Much has been said about the "vast wasteland" since Newton N. Minow, chairman of the Federal Communications Commission, used the term in his speech of May 9, 1961. But the top spokesmen of the networks waited their time before making major replies. Then, quite by coincidence, two of the most influential men in the television industry spoke on the same evening—December 7, 1961. While Frank Stanton, president of the Columbia Broadcasting System, was delivering the Benjamin Franklin Lecture at the University of Pennsylvania, Robert W. Sarnoff, chairman of the National Broadcasting Company, was speaking before the National Broadcasting Company Television and Radio Affiliates in Beverly Hills, California, on the occasion of NBC's thirty-fifth anniversary of the founding of the broadcasting network. Both speeches were vigorous affirmations of television's sense of responsibility to the public. Mr. Stanton and Mr. Sarnoff welcomed public criticism of television programing; both expressed concern, however, over the possibility of governmental intervention in the communications media. Said Mr. Sarnoff:

> When criticism comes—pointedly and suggestively—from the voice of governmental authority, speaking softly but carrying a big hint, at what point does criticism become coercion— where does freedom leave off and interference begin? One answer was suggested by the French dramatist Corneille when he wrote: "For someone who can do as he pleases, to entreat is to command."

Neither speaker referred to Mr. Minow by name. But the speeches were patently direct replies to the charge of May 9, and perhaps anticipations of the FCC hearings scheduled for January 1962. In an address before the Commonwealth Club in San Francisco on December 22, 1961, Mr. Minow remarked that "enough—perhaps too much—has been said about the wasteland of television." He suggested that we turn our thoughts to "the promised land—the second decade of nation-wide television."

[3] Text furnished by E. K. Meade, Jr., vice president of the Columbia Broadcasting System, with permission for this reprint.

[4] For biographical note, see Appendix.

Mr. Stanton's lecture contained an analysis of what he called "the substance of television—its programing." And he offered a lively defense of diversity:

> Should we meet the standards set by *most* of the people *all* of the time? I think that the answer to that is clearly no. We must be constantly aware that ours is a most varied population, with a wide range of degrees of sophistication, of education, of interests, of tastes. We must make an effort to accommodate that endless variety. But we must do it with some sort of scale and balance in mind.

Moreover, he said that he did not know

> any satisfactory or democratic alternative to letting the people set the standards of programing by the simple act of accepting or rejecting what is offered. . . . The public verdict is . . . the safest and surest, the most valid and most enduring.

Linking his theme with the early prospect of international television, Mr. Stanton remarked

> If we are to go before the world with an influential voice in the solution of problems inevitable with the coming of international television, we must have the clear conviction that so far as we are concerned we are willing to abide by the verdict of the people and refuse to look for salvation to any authority.

There is no more appropriate figure in all history with whom to associate a discussion of communications than Benjamin Franklin. His many-sided genius, touching with equal effectiveness upon printing, diplomacy, science, legislation and philosophy, would be fully at home in our age. The scientific achievements of this century would captivate his inquisitive mind. Its surging political restlessness would invite his clear-sighted wisdom. Its social innovations would enkindle that unmatched vitality that we prize as the very heart of Franklin's personality.

Franklin was the great empiricist of the American experience, epitomizing that vein of practicality that ran all through our early history and that sought, with unapologetic directness, to express ideals in propositions that worked. The preoccupation of his long life was, not with a vain search for the abstractly perfect, but with an exhilarating quest for the best that was workable. This it was that gave him his essential optimism and his unique character, too, as a sparkling prototype of the twentieth century man.

No aspect of this century, I think, would have challenged Franklin's interest more than the advances that it has made in communications—and, among these, none more than television. Here is a medium bringing the sights and sounds of every area of life into 90 per cent of America's 52 million homes. Here is a medium obliged, by its nature, to provide something for everybody in a heterogeneous nation of 185 million people. Here is a medium calling for resources of untold millions of dollars, unprecedented in communications, to support it. Here is a medium as fraught with the public interest as printing was in Franklin's day, and to which freedom is as vital. Here is a medium on the verge of directly linking together all the continents of a troubled and divided world.

Towards the close of his invaluable services to the American cause during the Revolution, Franklin looked plaintively towards world order: "I hope," he wrote, "that mankind will at length, as they call themselves reasonable creatures, have reason and sense enough to settle their differences without cutting throats." Coupled with this hope was his lifelong faith in the power of communication. As a boy of seventeen, he took over the editorship of the *New England Courant,* when his brother, the editor, went to jail for criticizing authority; as an old man in his seventies, he undertook long and arduous journeys to bespeak his country's cause overseas. There is every reason to believe that the practical mind of Franklin would have seen world-wide communications as a promising instrument for achieving world order.

Today television is very nearly at the beginning of its international era. It has, I think, an enormous potential contribution to make towards world order. But American television faces that era with many unresolved problems. It is, of course, inevitable that a medium that has grown so fast should create unique problems just as it has presented unique opportunities.

Some of them are transitory in nature. Some are fundamental. In an impatient society, hard pressed with the ugly potentials of a cold war, these fundamental problems can invite dangerously precipitous solutions, superficially attractive perhaps but full of land mines.

Chief among these fundamental problems is the arrival at standards for programing. Whose standards should they be?

How should they be determined? Can you trust the people to know what is good for them? Or must they be told by some authority? I want to discuss this problem against the total context—social, cultural, economic and political—in which television must function, and against the background of a free society that has been particularly alert to abridgments of the freedom of communications—whether of the press, of speech, of assembly, or of any extension of these that technical developments since the Bill of Rights have made possible.

I am aware that this subject moves far from the role of communications in world order. But I am sure you will agree that we must have a clearer understanding of television here at home before we can help construct its role among nations.

The substance of television is, of course, its programing. The sources of the programs available to nearly all the 550 commercial television stations in the United States are manifold. They may be produced by the broadcaster. They may be acquired by the broadcaster from outside producers. Or they may be transmitted to a station directly from a network with which the station enters into a contractual agreement. The network, in turn, produces some of its programs, including virtually all its news, and acquires others from outside sources. Almost all commercial stations have an affiliation with one or more networks. Such a relationship is, not only voluntarily assumed, but eagerly sought by the stations, which acquire from the networks a little over half of their total programing, including most of their national and international news.

The volume and variety of programing produced by the three television networks are, I think, wholly without precedent in the history of communications. In the month of November, for example, the three networks provided their affiliates with over a thousand hours of programing. This consisted chiefly of 99½ hours of actual news events and straight news broadcasts, 23¾ hours of documentary news, 19 hours of discussion, 45 hours of education and religion, 77 hours of sports, 63¼ hours of general drama, 8 hours of panel shows, 84 hours of situation comedy, 41½ hours of variety, 84¾ hours of serial drama, and 74¾ hours of children's programs. Of the total, 56 hours were mysteries and 60½ hours were westerns—a combined total of 11 per cent of all the programing.

The range of subjects and material that appeared on the three networks in November was extremely wide. There were biographical studies of such diverse men as U. S. Grant and Vincent Van Gogh, Al Smith and Sinclair Lewis. There were several special half-hour biographies of Speaker Sam Rayburn. There were long reports on such countries as Germany, Spain, Yugoslavia, and France. There were interviews with men representing a provocative cross section of the world today: Prime Minister Nehru, Igor Stravinsky, Hugh Gaitskell, John Kenneth Galbraith, Bertrand Russell. Full-length dramatic productions included Hans Conreid and Jane Wyatt in "Little Lost Sheep," Julie Harris in "Victoria Regina," and Fred Astaire in "Moment of Decision."

It is true, of course, that much of the television fare of the month was light. But most fiction published every month is light reading. It is relevant to remember, too, that of the hundreds of popular magazines published in this country, only four are news magazines and only four more are of generally serious editorial content. And many Sunday newspapers, with from sixteen to eighteen pages devoted to sports and amusements, have a single page devoted to editorials and a single column to education.

The press in this country, nevertheless, is carrying out its responsibilities far better than that of any other country and better than it ever has before, given the economic and social context in which it must function. Newspapers and magazines must attract and hold their readers. They must attract and hold their advertisers. They have arrived at patterns of content after a good deal of tough trial and error. They are not, of course, an exact parallel to television, for they are not subject to licensing; most publications, however, are objects of partial government subsidy through advantageous postal rates.

Like the magazines and newspapers, television fills a dual role of entertaining and informing, diverting and instructing, relaxing and stimulating. There are those, I am sure, who would have television exclusively informative and instructive. There are those, too, who would have it exclusively entertaining and diverting. But the economic demands of the medium and the capacities and interests of human beings require it to be both.

As a matter of practical economic necessity, television has had to evolve as an entertainment medium in order to support its other roles. But there is more to it than that. Television is an extremely vivid, incisive medium. A picture's being worth a thousand words is a hoary aphorism, but it has new force when applied to television. If the medium were used entirely, or even primarily, for information, it would so dilute its effectiveness, in that role, that it would defeat its own purpose. You cannot feed people a steady diet of gravity and crisis and not sacrifice emphasis and the ability to engage and hold their attention.

On the other hand, the entertainment role of television has many aspects. Entertainment is a highly subjective thing. From time immemorial, while some men have delighted in tales of high adventure and mystery, others have been more diverted by provocative dramas of emotional or social conflict. Others like comedies. Still others care nothing about imagined situations and like interesting personalities or variety shows, or sports events.

Despite this diversity of taste, somebody has to set standards. Broadcasters have turned to the general public. In the absence of the kind of physical circulation that publications have to measure their public acceptance, there is a nation-wide rating service to provide the networks with means of determining public acceptance of programs. This does not mean that no network would broadcast a program that does not attract a high rating. This is obviously not so, since year after year many important broadcasts, particularly of an informational character, do go on the air in spite of consistently low ratings.

In October, for example, the CBS television network broadcast the first of a series of three hour-long interviews with General Eisenhower on the problems of the presidency. The first was universally acclaimed by the critics. It was on the air in prime evening time. Its rating indicated that some 6 million people saw the broadcast as compared to 21 million who tuned to the suspense drama and 26 million to the popular song program that were on the air at the same time on the other two networks.

Now there are several ways that you can look at that figure, 6 million. Compared to the audience of a popular entertainment television show, it is small. Compared to the audience of a best-selling book, whether informative or escape fiction, it is gigantic. Compared to the largest metropolitan newspapers, it ranges from three to ten times their daily circulation. Now consider what an hour-long discussion is equal to in terms of the written word. It is about nine thousand words—twenty-seven typed pages. So the real gauge of public interest in what General Eisenhower had to say on the problems he faced as President can be judged by the fact that more people, by many times over, were exposed to twenty-seven pages of comment on serious matters than read any newspaper, or any best seller. We broadcast a second conversation with General Eisenhower on Thanksgiving night, and we are scheduled to broadcast another early in 1962.

On December first, last Friday, the CBS television network broadcast a Young People's Concert of the New York Philharmonic in prime evening time. Although we knew that this concert would interest fewer viewers than "Rawhide," which it displaced that evening, we believed that there was enough following of good serious music in America to justify the experiment of making such a distinguished orchestra available to the family in prime time. As it turned out, forty times as many people heard the Philharmonic that night as heard it during the entire season at Carnegie Hall last year. But we were certainly not under any illusion that there would be more than sing along with Mitch every week.

This illustrates, I think, the kind of perplexing questions that are evoked by the phrase "meeting the standards set by the people." Should we meet the standards set by *most* of the people *all* of the time? I think that the answer to this is clearly no. We must be constantly aware that ours is a most varied population, with a wide range of degrees of sophistication, of education, of interests, of tastes. We must make an effort to accommodate that endless variety. But we must do it with some sort of scale and balance in mind. For the second perplexing question is: At what point should a mass medium stop moving towards the interests of a relative few? How few is the "relative few"?

I think that it would be a misuse of the airwaves, for example, to carry very esoteric, avant-garde material that experienced observers know would be meaningless to all but a handful of the initiated. On the other hand, there is a great and restless potential in the American people to broaden their cultural horizons. Television can, and does, play an enormous role in stimulating that potential. I don't think, however, that these stirrings are visited upon all of the people, or even most of them, at the same time. And so we have to experiment. We know pretty clearly, after a reasonable trial, when a program of popular entertainment registers with the people. We assume that if it does, they are entitled to see it and we ought to continue it. We assume that if a vast majority of the people vote against it, we ought to discontinue it and try something else.

But we also know about this thirst for new things that I speak of—the appetite for new entertainment or new cultural experiences. We try to meet that, too, by interpolating in our schedule things which we are not at all certain that enough people want to justify use of a mass medium, but which we think enough might be interested in seeing. We watch very carefully how the people react, because their acceptance or rejection influences our next move—and ought to influence it.

I don't know any satisfactory or democratic alternative to letting the people set the standards of programing by the simple act of accepting or rejecting what is offered. It has been said that the public is getting no choice of kinds of television fare, but with rare exceptions in the schedules this is simply not the case. It has also been said—contradictory as it may sound—that television is ruled by two tyrannies: the tyranny of the majority, and the tyranny of the mercantilists; that, on the one hand, its sole purpose is to drug the great mass of citizens and, on the other hand, it is the tool exclusively of greedy men who will foist anything on the public if it will serve their purpose in selling things that nobody wants. I realize that there is a great deal of emotion in both these charges. But they are not uncommon and we ought to take a look at them.

The tyranny of the majority is, of course, a classical dilemma of the democratic state. It has been asserted from ancient times that it leads to a rule of mediocrity, or even of the lowest common denominator. It seems to me that the American political experience—and I believe also the American social and cultural experiences—have minimized this danger by a widely respected recognition of the rights and interests of minorities. Indeed, in our own time, the advancement of such recognition has been a major preoccupation of our civil history. And culturally, we evolved, from the beginning, institutions and media to serve the interest of scores of intellectual minorities.

The unique problem in this respect with regard to television is that, both because of the technical limitations on the number of channels and because of the economic demands of the medium, it is impossible to have separate channels to serve every worthwhile minority whatever its size. For example, in periodicals, there is no general uprising because a popular weekly does not publish an essay in praise of Spenser, for there are several specialized publications that would. In the case of television, we must remain primarily the servant of the majority but at the same time recognize the interests and values of significant minorities. We have to serve both. Thus, the CBS television network has the weekly program, "Accent," with the poet John Ciardi as host, which is concerned with the arts and occasionally also with specialized aspects of science and education, but it must keep the program away from the esoteric or cabalistic.

Television is concerned with the relative size of cultural minorities, because television has a primary responsibility to serve more than quantitatively minute minorities. It is unlikely that we will do anything to stimulate discussion of the use of classical images in early eighteenth century poetry—although I am quite sure that somewhere there are several passionately dedicated students of the subject. But we would do something about the general subject of art in American life, even though an overwhelming share of the audience is not interested.

Television does, in fact, have a variety of programs that are, while directed hopefully at the majority, seeking to meet standards of excellence in substance or in manner acceptable to the most demanding minority. In looking over the highlights for this month, for example, on the stations here in Philadelphia, I see these, which no one, by the wildest stretch of the imagination, can charge to catering only to the majority—although I hope a majority will be tempted to watch them.

On Sundays, Philadelphians, whatever their interests, will be able to see, among others:

Interviews with Pearl Buck, the late Frank Lloyd Wright, Harry Emerson Fosdick and David Ben-Gurion.

Such dramas as Ben Hecht's "Notorious."

The memorable film production of "The Wizard of Oz."

A series from the University of Michigan on American folklore.

A profile biography of Wendell Willkie.

A study of jazz.

Ballets, including "Hansel and Gretel" and "The Nutcracker Suite."

On Christmas Eve, the opera "Amahl and the Night Visitors," the oratorio "The Messiah," and the play "The Other Wise Man."

Nor is this merely a "Sunday ghetto" in the midst of tawdry weekday programing. Three ballets performed at the Rodin Museum will be broadcast on a Monday night; a documentary on the problem of school dropouts on a Tuesday night; "The Picture of Dorian Gray" on a Wednesday night; "A Conversation with Walter Lippmann" on a Thursday night; an original drama, "Come Again to Carthage," on a Friday night; a musical program, "The Enchanted Nutcracker," on a Saturday night.

We all know that many of these programs will not attract a large share of the viewers watching television at the time that they are on the air. They, and others like them, are broadcast because the interests of significant minorities are recognized by broadcasters. But the broadcasters are thoroughly justified, under any principles of cultural democracy, in basing such recognition to some extent on reasonable assurance that the program is not so specialized as virtually to black out the station. In fact, responsible programing should have the opposite effect and invite the many to come in with the interested few—and get something out of it.

The blanket charge that the trouble with television is that it permits the tyrannizing of the public by the manufacturers of consumer goods and their advertising agencies—in league with the broadcasters and in contempt of any except mercantile values —seems to me to impede any useful discussion. We live in a mercantile society, and our material life is based on the sale and purchase of goods and services. This is not unique to our century or to our land. The development of mercantilism has coincided in modern history with the development of democracy —not because it was a philosophic ideal but because it worked best, even if imperfectly, with democratic institutions. The reason, of course, is that, for all its faults, mercantilism is not categorical, not authoritative. It is open-ended and gives room to move around economically; and, without that, political democracy would be meaningless in practical life.

It flowed inevitably from this that unsubsidized newspapers and magazines should so structure their special economies that they could earn their way by serving the general economy of which they are part. Radio did the same thing—not inventing the relationship but necessarily following it. And so has television. These media could not hit upon a kind of financial structuring wholly out of tune with the rest of the economy. No one ever has. In ecclesiastical societies, art and music were supported by the church and were in substance church-oriented. In the periods of economic extremes, they were supported by rich patrons. Communications and expression generally have always been both in and of their social systems.

Now the special nature of television has, of course, introduced problems that the magazines and newspapers did not face in their relationship to the sources of their economic support— the advertisers. But these are gradually being resolved and anyone who makes a serious inquiry into it will find that the contrast between the advertiser-program relationship in early radio and that in television today is incredibly revealing. Radio often in those days merely sold time which was filled by the advertiser. Outside of news, radio originated little but sustaining programs. Today television is decisively concerned with the programing, originating much of it and then finding advertisers interested in sponsoring it.

But in the final analysis, all this is a digression, because the advertiser has no immunity from the verdict of the public. Every time his program is on the air, it is submitted to the viewer's vote. If it lost or never attained that vote, it would go off the air with absolute inevitability. And so again we get back to the fundamental question: Should it be the public or should it be some authority—whether in the government or a czar in the industry or some independent commission—that makes the verdict?

The public verdict is, I have no doubt, the safest and surest, the most valid and most enduring, one. But it has its price. It is less swift and less efficient, but it shares such limitations with all other procedural aspects of the democratic life. We in America have over and over again faced that particular dilemma, and we have refused to put a premium on speed and efficiency at any cost. To advocate that there is a price for speed and efficiency that we refuse to pay is not to advocate the status quo.

A decade from now, if the public verdict prevails, television will be unrecognizable from what we have today. The medium will change because there is a constant, slow but inevitable upward movement in the standards and interests and capacities of a free people. If this were not so, the American experience would be meaningless, for life consists in growth. If we say that it is not so, if we start making exceptions, we are losing faith in the democratic dynamic. If we liken the mass of people and their ability to make their own decisions to unsupervised children and their desire for a constant diet of sweets, we are striking at the heart of what a democracy is all about—that the people, whatever their temporary errors or inadequacies, are, in the long run, the best judges of their own interests, and that they will make themselves heard.

In a pluralistic society like ours there are a great many additional built-in safeguards against persistent excesses. These are far more effective over the long haul than paternal authority. The variety of pressures that make themselves felt in such a society—civic organizations, academic groups, churches, the newspapers, articulate and forceful individuals—are the indirect influences that set the pace for the evolution of culture in a democracy. The important thing is that essential freedom remains —there is freedom to yield to pressures or to resist them, to respect those that seem enlightened and to ignore those that seem self-serving, to make mistakes, to take risks. All this takes time, and all this involves the chance of error. But there is no finality about it. And *that* is the rub with any pressure stemming from authority. The pressures normal in a democracy say, "You should." The pressure of authority says, "You shall."

We have also on the side of the public verdict the continued rise in the educational level of the people: they are better qualified each year to make the verdict. Isn't this—and not salvation by authority—our real, in fact our only, hope? Let me be precise. I don't think that you could get many more people to look at a discussion program on political theory by arranging it so that there was nothing else to look at during the program except other discussions. This kind of forced feeding not only smacks of the dictatorial but probably wouldn't work. People would simply not look at television just as they do not, in great numbers, read learned quarterlies. They would find their diversion elsewhere. It is our job as a mass medium to build a following and move ahead generally at its pace, while at the same time attempting an acceleration through new directions in programing.

Is it possible for television, because it is more ubiquitous and more immediate and more vivid than other mass media, to have a wholly different content? I don't believe that it is. I think that it must make available to its audience what the latter has shown that it expects of the media serving the millions. If it doesn't it will just no longer be serving them. The material available on the television networks pretty much parallels, in kind, the material that characterizes such other mass media as the paperback book—the rise of which chronologically has matched that of television and which now sells 294 million copies annually. Reassuring as it is to know that you can get Plato's dialogues or Trevelyan's histories in inexpensive editions at Liggett's, it is still not surprising that Mickey Spillane remains the all-time best seller. Or that, of the 248 new titles in paperback fiction in the present fall season, 92, or 37 per cent, are westerns, adventures and mysteries. Or even that the majority of the other titles are obviously light romances and other escape fiction.

But I would think that a literary critic would be something less than perceptive if he picked up the first fifty titles and used them as a base for a report on the achievement of the American novel. I would question also the judgment of an historian who concluded that a sound basis for appraising the role of the magazine in American life was to read indiscriminately every magazine that he found on the first shelf of his neighborhood newsstand. Such a method would be considered an aberration in critical methodology and its results could not be taken seriously.

But isn't this exactly what has happened in the case of television? The process by which it was concluded that television programing was "a vast wasteland" was described in these words: "Sit down in front of your television set when your station goes on the air . . . and keep your eyes glued to that set until the station signs off." A writer in a series for a magazine with a long history of westerns and mysteries, began with the same specious approach: "Arose at five-thirty . . . turned the family television set to Channel 5, sat down in front of it and stayed there until Channel 5 went off the air twenty hours later."

The danger of this kind of sensationalized and oversimplified approach, with its broad brush conclusions, is not only that it grotesquely distorts the situation as it is, a clear perception of which is necessary to improvement, but also that it invites impulsive measures directed at making fundamental changes on the ground that any change is a change for the better. Actually, the only change that I have seen suggested is that the government supervise programing by use of its licensing power and by regulating a major program source, the networks.

How much improvement can either of these really bring about? If government authority sets standards, qualitative or quantitative, for television programing, whose standards are they going to be? The chairman of a commission? A majority of a commission? A congressional committee?

You would have authoritative standards that would stifle creativity. You would have a rigidity that would discourage experimentation. You would have the subjective judgment of a small group imposed on the many. And you would have the constant danger of the misuse of the medium for political purposes.

"Experience should teach us," Justice Brandeis warned, "to be most on our guard to protect liberty when the government's purposes are beneficent. Men born to freedom are naturally alert to repel invasion of their liberty by evil-minded rulers. The greatest dangers to liberty lurk in insidious encroachment by men of zeal. . . ."

Television does need improving. So do private colleges and charitable organizations. So do motion pictures and magazines. So do typewriters and cameras. All these have improved immeasurably over the years, and they will improve further. But they did not improve because some central authority said they must. They improved because they had elbowroom to move forward in response to the demands put upon them and the new opportunities that new conditions brought them.

It has been suggested that, because we are in a deadly serious conflict with the forces of communism all over the world, there is no time for the slow evolutionary processes of democracy, and that the government ought, therefore, to "do something" about our television programing. This seems to me an illogical and dangerous example of what George Orwell called "unthinking." Even the most violent critics of television have commended the job that it has done on national and international affairs. All this would go down the drain if there were a widespread conviction among Americans that such programs were conditioned by government directives.

Overseas, the effect would be equally damaging. The control of the substance of the communications media—always in its early stages under the mask of "guidance"—has long been the first step in totalitarianism. The world has been too painfully aware of this not to be suspicious, justly or not, of such a move here. We ought rather to be facing this world conflict by strengthening our freedoms. The only way to do that is to reaffirm our faith in the judgment of the people, not to abandon it.

If we do not have free television here, how can we possibly advance any advocacy of freedom of international television before the world? We certainly cannot believe that international television can effectively contribute towards the establishment of world order if it is *not* free—if it is to be merely a crushing maelstrom of rival governmental propaganda, seeking to drown each other out. If we are to go before the world with an influential voice in the solution of problems inevitable with the coming of international television, we must have the clear conviction that so far as we are concerned we are willing to abide by the verdict of the people and refuse to look for salvation to any authority.

I am not in sympathy with the soft inclination to turn the content of any medium over to governmental control on the grounds that to insist on the rights of a new medium will obscure the rights of the older. Whether it is apparent on the surface or not, the freedoms of all media are interlocked. If our culture, with all its imperfections, is to remain free of state determinism, our communications media must remain free. If our thought, our speech and press are to remain free, television, with all the other media, must remain free. Basic freedoms are not divisible, to be rationed out discriminately. No one who has read Franklin can possibly imagine that the author of "An Apology for Printers" would agree that if an utterance were reproduced on paper it should be free, but if it were reproduced on tape, or film, or the face of a tube, it should not.

It is no less delusive to suggest that there are limitations on freedom stemming from the purpose of the content of a medium. Does anyone believe that because a book or a magazine or certain pages of a newspaper entertain rather than inform, they should be less free? I do not think it would be of any use in the development of our free society if all our news and informational media were wholly free and all other expression were subject to government regulation, for the character of any people is formed by powers rooted deep in *all* areas of expression. In the report of the Commission on Freedom of the Press, Professor William Ernest Hocking said:

Neither the value nor the duty of expression is limited to its more purposeful aspects. Speech and press may be trivial, casual, emotional, amusing, imaginative, speculative, whimsical, foolish; all utterance serves a social end—to report to fellow beings mutual presence and interest, the play of mood, the vagaries of taste, the gropings for principle, the barometric flux of belief and disbelief, hope and fear, love and hate, and thus to shape attitudes. . . . There is a common duty to protect the whole range of this freedom, as a right of social existence.

Are we so bereft of that trust in the people so magnificently exemplified by Franklin's age that we must now turn over the substance of the most promising medium we have to the control of government because the people do not know what is good for them? Are we going to be incapable of extending freedom of communications abroad in the interests of world order, because we can find no alternative to diminishing it at home?

I think not. As we look to this challenge, peculiarly of our time, the hopeful spirit of Franklin beckons from history. The printer of Philadelphia would contemplate the future of this great new medium with optimism, not despair; with confidence, not fear; with patience, not anxiety. We cannot do less if we are to realize opportunities as boundless in our age as the stubborn quest for freedom was in Franklin's.

REFLECTIONS ON THE DILEMMAS
OF OUR TIME

THE CONTINUING EFFECT OF THE
AMERICAN REVOLUTION [1]

ARNOLD J. TOYNBEE [2]

Dr. Arnold J. Toynbee is one of the world's most erudite historians. Like all men who have lots of ideas—especially provocative ideas—he is also a controversial figure. Students and teachers who read the following address will find in it many themes for lively, perhaps even bitter, controversy. Dr. Toynbee would doubtless rejoice in such a circumstance because he likes discussion and other civilized talkfests.

"The Continuing Effect of the American Revolution" was delivered at the eighteenth-century Capitol of Colonial Williamsburg, Williamsburg, Virginia, on June 10, 1961. A passage from Winthrop Rockefeller's opening statement on a similar occasion in 1960 will set the scene. Indicating that his father's interest in the restoration of Colonial Williamsburg went deeper than "the reconstruction of eighteenth-century buildings alone" and embraced the concept that "the future may learn from the past," Mr. Rockefeller said:

> As part of this concept and to make certain that an important chapter of our history is not forgotten, we celebrate each year the fifty days from May 15 to July 4. In the year 1776 these days formed an important Williamsburg period we know as the Prelude to Independence. Many of the first steps toward our freedom were taken during that period. On May 15, 1776, the convention of delegates meeting here passed the Virginia Resolution for American Independence. This led directly to the Declaration of Independence in Philadelphia on July 4.
>
> The delegates assembled here also wrote a state constitution, and elected Patrick Henry as the first governor of Virginia.
>
> And it was here on June 12, 184 years ago that the Virginia Declaration of Rights was unanimously adopted.

Dr. Toynbee's address set forth an Englishman's observations on America's role in world affairs. Specifically, he asserted that "it is open to her [the United States] to take the lead again in the American

[1] Text furnished by Donald J. Gonzales, vice president of Colonial Williamsburg. Reprinted by permission of Dr. Toynbee and Mr. Gonzales.

[2] For biographical note, see Appendix.

Revolution in its present world-wide stage." Then he inquired: "Will she take, as her measure of success, the quantity, per head, of material goods consumed at home, instead of measuring her success by the quantity of fundamental material and spiritual needs that she can help the still indigent majority of mankind to satisfy?"

In the course of his argument, Dr. Toynbee suggested that the "destiny of our Western civilization turns on the issue of our struggle with all that Madison Avenue stands for more than it turns on the issue of our struggle with communism." So instead "of spending our earnings on unwanted consumer goods for ourselves, why not spend them on meeting the basic and pressing needs of the majority of our fellow human beings?" Believing that the majority's struggle to achieve equality is "by far the most important movement in the world today," Dr. Toynbee said "the cue for us, the hitherto privileged minority, is to be patient, and to concentrate on doing our best to help the majority of our fellow human beings to achieve the equality that comes first in their order of priorities."

When Dr. Toynbee predicted that it was "a very controversial thing" to link the destiny of Western civilization with what "Madison Avenue" stands for, he engaged in understatement. Many top executives have entered vigorous refutations of his charge, and have spoken of advertising's significant role in the development of our mass-consumption economy. Among the speeches that interested students may wish to examine are the following: "How to Sell America Instead of Giving It Away," delivered before the Economic Club of Detroit on November 6, 1961, by Charles H. Brower, president of Batten, Barton, Durstine & Osborn; "Responsibility—Keynote of the Sixties," delivered before the San Francisco Advertising Club on November 29, 1961, by Norman H. Strouse, president of the J. Walter Thompson Company; "Is Advertising Coming of Age?" delivered before a meeting of the American Association of Advertising Agencies in Coronado, California, on October 17, 1961, by Edwin Cox, chairman of the executive committee of Kenyon and Eckhardt; and "Advertising, the Multiplier of Our Economy," given at a meeting of the Association of National Advertisers in Hot Springs, Virginia, on November 2, 1961, by Roy E. Larsen, chairman of the executive committee of Time, Inc.

This is the second successive year in which a distinguished Englishman has kindly consented to the reprinting of an address delivered in America. Dr. Toynbee's speech follows that of Sir Charles Percy Snow, whose "Moral Un-Neutrality of Science" appeared in REPRESENTATIVE AMERICAN SPEECHES: 1960-1961.

Here in Williamsburg today we are celebrating the eve of the American Revolution in the moment of pregnant silence before the firing of the shot heard round the world. It was a generous act of yours to invite an Englishman—and not your first English speaker; Sir Pierson Dixon has preceded me—to be your speaker on this historic occasion. I am as much touched by the honor that you have done me as I was when I was invited, as I once was, not long ago, to be the speaker at the celebration of India's independence day in the city of Hyderabad, Deccan. Perhaps, after all, my British nationality is not a disqualification. It is true and obvious, of course, that Britain was the first country to oppose the Revolution and was also the first to learn by experience that to oppose the Revolution is to court defeat. Yet it is also true, though perhaps not so well remembered, that Britain, besides being the first country to lose by the American Revolution, was at the same time the first country, after America herself, to gain by it.

The Revolutionary War was a civil war, and this on both sides of the Atlantic. In Britain, as well as in America, it bore the fruits of reform, release, and rejuvenation. The liberal movement that the American Revolution launched in Britain in the 1780's was temporarily arrested through tragically coming into conflict with another revolution that was set in motion, this time in France, by one of the early echoes of the sound of the American shot. Yet, after the Napoleonic Wars, reform in Britain gathered momentum again. It came to political fruition there in the Reform Bill of 1832; and after the two world wars it has come to social fruition in the present-day British welfare state. History never comes to a halt in Britain or in America or anywhere else; and we may be sure that history will continue to flow and to bring changes in its course unless, of course, mankind deliberately wipes itself off the face of this planet in a third world war which this time will be fought with atomic weapons.

I have the impression—and I think I am right—that contemporary America does not much like the contemporary British welfare state. Yet this twentieth century semisocialist dispensation in Britain is one of the children of the eighteenth-century American Revolution. It often happens that one's children turn out differently from one's expectations and one's desires. Yet it is quite useless to try to disown an unwanted child. Paternity is a fact that has to be faced. By now, the eighteenth-century American shot has indeed been heard all round the world. The Revolution has become world-wide, and the Old World, as well as the New World, is swarming with the American Revolution's progeny. The Russian, Chinese, Egyptian, Congolese, and Cuban revolutions display, unmistakably, their origins in the parent revolution in this country. And, at the moment, America's comment on this practical joke that destiny has played upon her seems to me to be fairly expressed in Queen Victoria's words: "We are not amused."

How much of what is manifest today was foreseen by the Founding Fathers? Those great men were, of course, all agreed in working together for one objective that was immediate and definite. They were working for complete self-government for the thirteen colonies; and this political claim of theirs was based on precedent. They were claiming for themselves the political rights that the people of England had successfully asserted in the course of the preceding century, first in the English Civil War and then in the Revolution of 1688. Thus, in the light of its immediate objective, the American Revolution might perhaps qualify for being labeled as a conservative movement, as indeed might the foregoing revolutions in England and in the Netherlands. As the Revolutionary leaders saw it, they were vindicating particular established rights. In their view the innovators were, not they, but the royal governments against which they were up in arms. This was their case as a lawyer might present it, and in the two seventeenth-century English revolutions, as in the eighteenth-century American Revolution, lawyers played a prominent part. But law is never able to catch more than a part of life in its net; the more important and more vital part usually defies and escapes legal definition. When one sets oneself a near and limited objective, it sometimes happens that one opens up a more distant and more general one. In asserting their hereditary constitutional rights for themselves, the eighteenth-century revolutionaries incidentally asserted human rights for all human beings and the right of self-determination for all peoples. We just now heard Mr. Carroll in his splendid recitation of the Virginia Declaration of Rights where the first two words of Article I are "all men"—all men, the whole human race; not just Virginians, not just Americans—but *all* men. These universal claims were incidental to the American revolutionaries' immediate constitutional object. But, when the immediate object had been achieved, as it had been within the seven years 1776-

1783, the universal elements in the American Revolution went rolling on with an elemental impetus. These universal claims were not confined by legal precedents. Their field was, and is, as boundless as time and space. They are still rolling on today. At this moment, for instance, they are inspiring men and women of African race in Alabama, in South Africa, in Angola. When one fires a shot, one cannot tell how far the sound is going to carry, or how many hearts will be roused to action by the echoes of it.

The Founding Fathers were united in the pursuit of their immediate constitutional aim, but they spoke individually with different voices about the universal issues that their revolution had opened up. One at least of the more prominent among them—not a Virginian, but John Adams—seems to have felt that the quantum of revolution which had sufficed to liberate the United States from British rule was as much as he wanted. John Adams lived to witness, and to castigate, the Jacobin phase of the French Revolution. By contrast, Jefferson seems to have taken pleasure in the thought that the disease of revolution is catching; and, consistently with this, he prescribed occasional bouts of political turbulence as being good medicine for the political health of mankind. There was, of course, a touch of humor in those sly observations of Jefferson's. All the same, we should probably be misreading his mind if we were to dismiss them as not having been meant to be taken seriously. What would have been Jefferson's comments on the American-inspired revolutions that are so vigorously on the boil today all over the world outside the United States itself? I fancy that Jefferson would not have disowned these non-American revolutions as being un-American. I believe he would have contemplated them with a sympathetic and indulgent eye. I also believe that he might have yielded to the temptation to make comments about them which would have been calculated to shock and infuriate the John Adamses of our generation. Indeed, I am not sure that Jefferson, if he were alive at this moment, might not gleefully get himself into trouble with the Committee on Un-American Activities and perhaps with the FBI. And the John Birch Society would surely pillory Mr. Jefferson side by side with Mr. Eisenhower as a Communist.

Now the spirits of the Founding Fathers continue to accompany the American people on its pilgrimage along the corridors of time. And I suggest that we can state, in terms of the revolutionary American generation, the issue—possibly the most crucial one in all subsequent American history—on which the American people has to come to a decision in our generation. What is going to be America's reaction to America's own revolution now that this American-inspired revolution has become world-wide? America's choice between her two alternative possible responses is going—I am sure—to be crucial for America's destiny, because it is going to decide what America's relations are to be with the majority of the human race.

This majority is revolutionary-minded today because it is suffering not only a political injustice of the kind that provoked eighteenth-century Americans into fighting the Revolutionary War. The majority today is suffering social and economic injustice as well. Two thirds or three quarters of mankind are now still living only just above the starvation line, and are still frequently dropping below it. Is America going to offer herself to this hungry majority as their leader? It is open to her to take the lead again in the American Revolution in its present world-wide stage. And, if she decides to do this, she has it in her power to help these aspiring peoples to help themselves. She can help them, in the first instance, to raise their material standard of living. This is not an end in itself; it is a means towards helping them to raise their spiritual standard. But elementary material improvements are a necessary means towards this, because, without them, it is almost prohibitively difficult for the great depressed majority to develop its spiritual potentialities. The village must purify its water supply and pave its lanes before it can afford to build a school and endow a schoolmaster. Will the American people expend itself and its spiritual and material resources on promoting this world-wide revolutionary enterprise? Or will America decide to take the alternative course? Will she concentrate her efforts on trying to preserve the vested interests of the affluent minority of the human race? Will she take, as her measure of success, the quantity, per head, of material goods consumed at home, instead of measuring her success by the quantity of fundamental material and spiritual needs that she can help the still indigent majority of mankind to satisfy?

This is the question that is confronting America today. And this, I believe, involves for America the supreme question of to be or not to be. If America does take the lead in the American-born world revolution of our time, then she will continue to march in the van of mankind along the main high road of human destiny. On the other hand, if she were to make the great refusal, she would be sidetracking herself. She would be inviting destiny to pass her by. Indeed, she would be giving destiny no other choice. For, if America were to refuse to play this role, a dozen other lands would be vying with each other to snatch it. Russia and China would perhaps be the obvious first candidates, but they are by no means the only candidates in the field.

But why should America think of rejecting a role that is so obviously her manifest destiny? She might reject it for the reason that moved the young man with great possessions to go away sorrowful from his encounter with Jesus. The young man failed to bring himself to fulfill the condition on which Jesus was willing to accept him as His follower. He could not bring himself to sell all that he had and to give it to the poor. This demand is, indeed, an acid test of human nature. Even if one is professing to fulfill it, one may hold back from fulfilling it one hundred per cent, as the story of Ananias and Sapphira exemplifies. There have, however, been saints who have risen to the occasion completely. There have been examples of complete self-denial, in the service of Christ, in every Christian century from the first onwards. The particular example that is most relevant for us in the West today—because of an example that comes out of the West itself—is the one that was set us for all time in the twelfth century by Saint Francis of Assisi.

The social environment into which Saint Francis was born was the affluent middle-class way of life that is characteristic of present-day America and most of the other Western countries. Northern and central Italy has been the precocious seedbed of our modern Western civilization; and middle-class affluence made its appearance there about seven hundred years before it spread to other parts of an expanding Western world. Saint Francis' father had made a fortune in the wool trade, and he brought up his son to enjoy everything that money could buy. Saint Francis threw himself into these worldly enjoyments with zest, and then recoiled from them with equal vehemence. His experience of the pride of life left him unsatisfied; so he repudiated everything that his father's worldly success had showered upon him. His father was astonished and indignant. Saint Francis found understanding, sympathy, and support when he appealed to the local bishop. If this had happened somewhere in the present-day Western world, the frustrated and outraged successful businessman might have denounced the bishop as a Communist and have put the Christian Church on the spot as a treasonable organization which was the enemy of free economic enterprise. The issue in twelfth-century Assisi was the issue between vested interests and holy poverty which had been raised by Jesus in Palestine, more than eleven hundred years back, according to the Gospel story. The same issue, I think, is confronting us in the modern Western world today.

There are many Westerners today, and this on both sides of the Atlantic, who have responded individually to the Christian call for a voluntary renunciation of this world's goods. This call is heard by human beings at all times, but it sounds with redoubled force in the ears of the affluent, and, in our world today, these are probably more numerous than they have ever been anywhere. There are not only many Roman Catholic friars and monks and nuns of the Franciscan and other religious orders. There are also laymen, and, some of these, atheists or agnostics, who are devoting their lives self-sacrificingly to the service of their fellows. There always have been individuals who have risen to these heights. The question is whether this spiritual standard can become so prevalent, throughout a society, that it will become part of that society's normal way of life. Evidently this is much harder to achieve, and it is especially hard where there are powerful social interests and institutions that are deliberately doing their utmost to lead the society in just the opposite direction.

In the Western world of our day, the tempter's role, which in Saint Francis' personal history was played by the saint's father, is being played, towards our society as a whole, by everything we sum up under the name of Madison Avenue and all that this label stands for. A considerable part of our ability, energy, time, and material resources is being spent today on inducing us to do hard labor in order to find the money for buying material goods that we should never have dreamed of wanting if we had been left to ourselves. The first assault on the cupidity that is latent in everyone of us is made by Madison Avenue by finesse. The strategy is to try to captivate us without allowing us to become aware of what is being done to us. If this sly approach does not do the trick, Madison Avenue has further psychological weapons in its armory. If all else fails, it will resort to sheer bullying, and it will carry this, if necessary, to the third degree. Now this is the inner adversary with whom we have to contend. And, just because he assails us from within, he is more formidable than any external opponent. And often we externalize our opponent when he is really within us. I would suggest that the destiny of our Western civilization turns on the issue of our struggle with all that Madison Avenue stands for more than it turns on the issue of our struggle with communism. That is a very controversial thing to say.

How, then, are we to deal with this skillfully engineered besetting temptation to put our treasure in the acquisition of a maximum quantity of consumer goods? Let us begin by putting the ideal represented by Madison Avenue to the touchstone of the original American Revolution. I have already made the point that the immediate and superficial issues of the original American Revolution were constitutional, while its ultimate and underlying issues were spiritual: the spiritual objectives of freedom and justice for all men. It may be disputed how far these ultimate objectives were consciously present in the minds of some, at any rate, of the Founding Fathers. But it is certain, I think, that not one of the Founding Fathers was inspired by the aim of producing and disposing of the maximum quantity of consumer goods. The Virginia Declaration of Rights was a positive gold mine for me—nuggets for me which keep dropping into my mouth. You heard Mr. Carroll recite the word "frugality" as one of the sixteen points. Producing and disposing of the maximum quantity of consumer goods was not the purpose of the American Revolution. What is more, it is not, of course, the true end of man. It is not, and surely cannot be, a satisfying target for us to set up for ourselves as the supreme goal of human endeavors. If our generation does not eventually revolt against the present attempt to impose this objective upon it, it can be foreseen that our children or our children's children will revolt against it eventually.

Besides being unacceptable spiritually, this ideal is unsound economically. An economy that depends for its survival on an artificial stimulation of material wants seems unlikely to survive for very long in any case. The Madison Avenue economic regime might even break down as the nemesis of its own unsoundness, even before it is overthrown through being repudiated on spiritual grounds. The only sound basis for an economy is to harness it to supplying wants that are genuine. And, fortunately for the economy of the affluent Western world of our day, there is no scarcity of genuine needs in the present-day world as a whole. There are enough of these to keep the West's productive forces busy at full capacity, even if we carry automation as far as our immense technological ingenuity will go. The needs of the economically depressed two thirds or three quarters of the human race are not only genuine. They are primary needs— needs for food, shelter, and clothing. "Give us this day our daily bread" is a prayer that has become almost meaningless for the affluent minority because, for them, its fulfillment has become a matter of course. But the indigent majority still prays this prayer from the heart; for, from day to day, it cannot tell whether its daily bread will be forthcoming.

Let us suppose that the affluent Western minority were to reorient the aim of its economy to the new objective of meeting the elementary needs of the indigent majority. This would insure our economy's health and survival. I think it would also give greater satisfaction to the workers by whose hard labor our economy is kept going. There can be little or no satisfaction in hard labor if the product of it is applied to meeting artificially created wants which do not correspond even to any genuine desires, not to speak of genuine needs. Instead of spending our earnings on unwanted consumer goods for ourselves, why not spend them on meeting the basic and pressing needs of the majority of our fellow human beings? Should we not get greater satisfaction than we now get out of our economic exertions under a regime which applied the product to this unmistakably valuable purpose?

No doubt some people will reply that this question is academic. The Madison Avenue economic regime, they will point out, is a going concern. Whether good or bad, it has at least the practical convenience of being already in operation. To change over from the existing regime, based on a maximum domestic consumption of consumer goods, to a new regime based on a maximum contribution to foreign aid, would, it will be objected, require a major economic revolution. It is unrealistic, it will be said, to make a proposal in which a major economic revolution is involved.

I think this objection can be met by a realistic answer. It is an historical fact that, twice over within the span of a single lifetime, the Western peoples have turned their economy upside down to meet the demands of a world war. Today the West finds itself in a crisis of no lesser magnitude than either of the world wars. It is evidently in its power to make once again as great a revolution in its economic life as it has made twice already in the recent past. If I am right—and I speak here with diffidence as a foreigner—if I am right, this is what President Kennedy is urging the American people to do. We cannot yet foresee the extent of the response that Mr. Kennedy is going to call out; but we can see already that the answer to this question, whatever the answer may be going to be, will probably be momentous for America's future.

Let us imagine, for a moment, that Mr. Kennedy has won for his policy the full measure of support for which he is hoping. So far, he has been talking in terms, I think, of a one per cent quota of the total annual national product as a target at which the affluent countries should aim in setting the standard for their contributions to foreign aid. One per cent would be neither generous nor adequate if it were to be taken as a maximum. In order to salvage the indigent majority of mankind, the affluent minority will surely have to divert a much larger quota of its product than this to foreign aid from the superfluous task of meeting the frivolous economic demands of Madison Avenue. Let us suppose that the diversion of resources from the service of imaginary wants of our own to the service of our neighbors' genuine needs were eventually to be made on the grand scale. The question then naturally arises: Would this revolution in the Western world's economy bring with it a solution of the West's and the world's current problems?

Here let me remind you at once of a notable saying of Mr. Kennedy's. He has told us that the reason for giving foreign aid is that this is a good thing to do for its own sake. He has not held out the prospect of any ulterior reward. And it is indeed obvious that, insofar as foreign aid is given from self-interested political motives, as a mere move in the power game that is being played between the West and the Communist world, foreign aid will then defeat its own purposes. Interested motives are always transparent; and, when they are detected, their presence stifles the gratitude that would be felt by the recipients of benefactions if the aid were being given for its own sake exclusively. We must, then, take care not to count on the possibility that foreign aid may bring us direct returns in the shape of political good will and support. But might it not perhaps produce indirect political returns that would not only be valuable for us but would be desirable in themselves from the standpoints of the aided countries and of the world as a whole? Might not foreign aid foster the growth of democracy in the countries to which it was being given?

This would be a legitimate hope for us who believe, as we Westerners do most sincerely believe, that democracy has proved itself by experience to be the least unsatisfactory of all political regimes that have been devised so far. But we must be cautious in allowing ourselves to expect that this hope is likely to be realized. Democracy, in the sense of representative self-government, is, after all, a peculiar institution. Even in the West, it has been indigenous in only a few countries; and, even in these countries, it has taken ages of time, and successions of efforts and sacrifices to bring democracy to maturity. Democracy is difficult to achieve and to maintain, because it requires for its successful operation the active cooperation of a large contingent of able, experienced, and public-spirited citizens such as you, for your good fortune, had in this country on the eve of the Revolution. The supply of citizens of the kind that is democracy's lifeblood has never been sufficient even in the handful of countries in which democracy is indigenous and more or less effective. The lack of a sufficient number of citizens of the necessary kind will, I believe, turn out, on analysis, to have been the principal cause of democracy's failure in those recently liberated countries in which it has been tried without success.

It is worth noting that, in nearly all these countries, democracy has been the people's first choice for a new regime. Even in Russia and in China, communism has been the second choice only. Neither country acquiesced in a Communist regime till it had become convinced, by trial and error, that a previous attempt to operate a democratic regime was not practical politics for this country in existing circumstances. Communism is not, of course, the only possible political second string in the present-day world. In some countries that have had an unfortunate experience of trying to make democracy work, the government has been taken over, not by Communists, but by army officers. No doubt there are still other alternatives to democracy that will be tried in the course of the newly liberated countries' long and hard journey towards their common goal of taking their places effectively in the modern community of states. We in the West ought to appreciate, and sympathize with, these Asian, African, and Latin American countries' difficulties. It would be unimaginative and unwise, on our part, if we were to hold it against any of them that they have not succeeded, at the first attempt, in acclimatizing so foreign a political plant as our Western species of democracy is for most of them. Above all, we must not take the line that the continuance of our grant to them of foreign aid ought to be conditional on their being successful in making democracy work.

We must conclude, then, that the current world revolution cannot be counted on to bring with it a world-wide triumph of democracy within any foreseeable period of time. If this is the truth, we are left with the question: What is the goal towards which the world revolution is tending? The first objective on the agenda of the depressed majority of mankind is, I believe, not liberty but equality; or, short of that, some mitigation of the traditional inequality between the respective situations of the unprivileged masses and the privileged minority. The masses are, I believe, now bent on achieving this aim. For them, the message of the American shot heard round the world has been the glorious and exciting news that equality is their birthright and is attainable. The world's peasantry has now waked up to a realization of the possibility that their conditions of life can be changed for the better—and changed at least partly by their own action. This is a revolutionary change of outlook. For these peasants have never dreamed before of what they are dreaming of now. They have been living in a state of resignation since the date, some five thousand years ago, when their patient shoulders were first saddled with the load of a civilization whose amenities, up till now, have been a privileged minority's monopoly. I believe that this first aim of the hitherto depressed majority is going to be attained. If and when this happens, we may hope that the objective of liberty may then come to the fore as the next item on the majority's agenda. Meanwhile, the cue for us, the hitherto privileged minority, is to be patient, and to concentrate on doing our best to help the majority of our fellow human beings to achieve the equality that comes first in their order of priorities.

The majority's struggle to achieve equality is, as I see it, by far the most important movement in the world today. On any but the shortest view, it is vastly more important than the current power struggle and current ideological controversy between the Western and Communist camps. The two contending camps agree with each other in taking for granted their common preoccupation with their competition with each other. It looks to me as if both camps will have to revise this common outlook of theirs. I myself believe that the outcome of their struggle with each other is going to be inconclusive. I don't expect to see either power bloc succeed in dominating the whole world, or either ideology succeed in converting the whole world. Up till now, no empire has ever succeeded in making its domination literally world-wide, and no ideology or religion has ever yet fulfilled its mission of converting the whole human race. Buddhism, Christianity, and Islam, for instance, have each succeeded in converting large portions of the human race; yet today their adherents coexist on the face of the same planet. As for the would-be world-empires—the Chinese Empire and the Roman Empire, for instance—they have come and gone. And, now that mankind has entered the Atomic Age, these attempts to unify the world politically by force cannot be repeated. We could, of course, resort to war again, and could wage it, and would wage it with atomic weapons; but the result would be, not to unite the human race, but perhaps to liquidate it. If the human race is to survive in the Atomic Age, it is going to have to learn rapidly to live together on the face of this planet like a single family. But the world-wide political unity that is now imperative cannot, in the Atomic Age, be achieved by coercion. It can be achieved only by agreement.

The shot fired in 1776 has been head round the world with a vengeance. The sound has traveled far, and has evoked responses that were foreseen at the time by few, perhaps, of the Founding Fathers with the conspicuous exception of Jefferson. The world-wide effects of the American Revolution have now confronted the United States with a fresh crisis in her history. Is she going to rise to the occasion? All the world is awaiting America's answer expectantly. As a foreign observer, I feel that the only advice I can properly venture to give my American contemporaries is this. Respond to history's present challenge in Jefferson's spirit. In fact, I ought to take refuge behind the skirts of Jefferson's coattails because from the present American standpoint what I have been saying is, of course, slightly pink, though not from the point of view of George Mason, nor Patrick Henry, nor Jefferson himself. But respond to history with history's present challenge in Jefferson's spirit. If you take your inspiration from Jefferson, I think you can face the future with confidence and hope.

A SCIENTIFIC SOCIETY—THE BEGINNINGS

The 29th John Wesley Powell Lecture [3]

GLENN T. SEABORG [4]

Both scientists and humanists are eagerly exploring ways of informing the public of the impact of technical knowledge upon national policy. This is a difficult job. And the educational objective is not confined to the average man in the street; even the leaders who make the top decisions find themselves in a maze of scientific data the full meaning of which often escapes their understanding. Hence the need for technical advisers at the highest administrative levels. Commenting on this condition, Sir Charles Percy Snow said in his *Science and Government* that one of the strangest features of a modern industrialized society "is that the cardinal choices have to be made by a handful of men: in secret: and, at least in legal form, by men who cannot have a first-hand knowledge of what those choices depend upon or what their results may be."

"Science and technology are now part of the fabric of Government, industry, and business, and of our social institutions. The destinies of individuals and peoples are irrevocably associated, from day to day, with the growth and use of scientific knowledge." So spoke Dr. Glenn T. Seaborg in an address at Denver, Colorado, on December 27, 1961, at a meeting of the American Association for the Advancement of Science. A 1951 Nobel prize-winning chemist from the University of California at Berkeley and currently chairman of the Atomic Energy Commission, Dr. Seaborg said: "Our aim must be to use science to strengthen democracy, not weaken it; to expand the potential fulfillment of the individual, not decrease it." Admitting that our democracy during the past twenty years had ingested but not digested science, he declared that the process of assimilation required an identification of the "freedom of scientific inquiry with our political and other freedoms." Accordingly, the development of our new society—the scientific society— can most successfully be achieved through a realization that scientists and other intellectuals alike share a common heritage of truth-seeking.

John Wesley Powell was a man who stands large in the history of American science. He believed in the frontier, and

---

[3] Text furnished by Dr. Seaborg. Reprinted with the permission of Dr. Seaborg and the American Association for the Advancement of Science.

[4] For biographical note, see Appendix.

he lived on it vigorously and adventurously, whether exploring the Colorado or insisting upon good science policy in Washington. Powell was a man of great vision. He saw clearly how science and engineering could develop the vast potential of the West to help make ours a great nation. He understood the nature of science and technology, and his Geological Survey demonstrated the usefulness of properly administered Government science. It is with pride, therefore, that I speak in Powell's name, here in the West he knew so well.

As I prepared for this lecture and considered some of the developments in science since Powell's time, my thoughts drifted to personal reminiscence. I recalled that in this season twenty-one years ago, my colleagues and I were doing the experiment which resulted in the discovery of plutonium. Needless to say, my world has not been the same since. Nor has my experience been unusual. The same forces operating in my case have markedly altered the lives of many millions of people and, indeed, society itself. Allowing for the lack of perspective that accompanies our closeness to the events, it still seems most pardonable to judge the past two decades to be one of the most portentous periods in human history. And this has been made so by science and technology.

I believe these things to be true not alone because of the novel dilemma revolving about nuclear weapons and the very survival of modern civilization; but also because of the general scientific-technological progress most dramatically exemplified by the peaceful atom and space exploration.

What is perhaps more important in the long run, granted our ability to avert total nuclear war, is the fact that in these two decades science and technology have become a dominant force in our social order. Much has been written about the scientific society, usually in the future tense. I believe we are warranted in changing the tense to the present. Although it is in its infancy, the scientific society has arrived; it has crossed the threshold in its relationship to society as a whole.

Science and technology are now part of the fabric of Government, industry and business, and of our social institutions. The destinies of individuals and peoples are irrevocably associated, from day to day, with the growth and use of scientific knowledge.

As was to be expected, the birth of the new infant has not been an easy one. Nor will its development be untroubled. It seems clear that science and technology are the most powerful forces for material advancement unleashed by man. The changes these forces bring—and will continue to bring—run wide and deep through society. Men as a whole are not friendly to such changes and forces. But to scientists, these developments may seem clearer than to most men.

The conception of our infant scientific society can best be assigned to the Renaissance. At that time, men challenged authority and the dogma that had ruled for centuries, and questioned the nature of the universe and man's place in it. The spirit of questioning in the Western world occurred on many fronts—in religion and philosophy and political theory, in art and literature, and in science. One important result was the expression in the Declaration of Independence and the Bill of Rights of the Constitution of the idea of individual personal, political, and intellectual freedom as controlling in an organized society. The same forces that liberated men politically, and in other ways, also produced the scientific method. With the growth of freedom of inquiry and the development of techniques for discovery, there began an acceleration of our ideas about nature. And the knowledge gained became highly significant when translated by technologists into tools.

Through our privileged perspective, we can see that—given the conditions of the last five centuries—everything that has happened has been virtually inevitable. For the achievement by men of the right to search for truth was the critical breakthrough. When this right was established on a continuing basis, it was only a matter of time until bacteria were discovered, electricity identified, and nuclear fission revealed. In a word, modern scientific knowledge and its application are a consequence of the vigorous exercise of the freedoms that arose in Western Europe and America.

I should like to introduce my stock-taking of the twenty years now ending by recalling some personal experiences to illustrate, in an anecdotal way, something of the changes within science and its new relationships to society.

In the fall of 1940, I was a young chemist at the University of California. We had been trained to believe that a deep gulf ran between pure and applied science. I was "pure," of course, searching for knowledge for its own sake. We were also poor—a property which followed purity like the night the day. But, being pure, we could accept poverty in good grace and even with some pride. Our poverty, of course, pervaded our research operations. Research funds were almost unknown. We built as much of our own equipment as we could, or coaxed our more talented friends into helping with it. Laboratory space was hard to come by. I can recall, as a graduate student, adopting the squatter's rights technique to obtain some space in an abandoned and condemned old wooden structure. But these were the accepted conditions of research science in those days, and we were hardly aware that our difficulties were difficulties.

The Lawrence Radiation Laboratory was a new kind of thing on the scientific horizon. It gave us a foretaste of things to come in some fields. The equipment was huge—by 1939, there were two cyclotrons that were giants among scientific equipment. Scientists from a variety of fields found it profitable frequently to pool their talents in working with the cyclotrons and their products. In this way, many of us encountered the emerging concept of group research. The laboratory budget, mostly from private sources, was considered enormous for the time, although it might arouse some amusement today.

Of course, we were not unaware of what was happening in the world—of the war that had started, and of the power-mad dictator who was a threat to our ideals and who aspired to engulf humanity in his medieval social order. But, like many research scientists, I did not then relate my work very much to practical things, and certainly not to war.

Until 1940, my research had been concerned with the iden-tification—with J. J. Livingood, primarily—of new radioisotopes. In the spring of that year, Edwin M. McMillan and Philip H. Abelson opened the transuranium field with their brilliant discovery of element 93, neptunium. It is an interesting com-mentary on the thinking and the priorities of the time that McMillan, who had started work aimed toward the discovery of the next higher element—element 94—was called away to do defense research on radar at the Massachusetts Institute of Technology.

With the assent of McMillan, three of us, my associate, the late Joseph W. Kennedy, Arthur C. Wahl, at that time a graduate student, and I, undertook to continue the research. It seems doubtful that many theses have been written that contained significance to rival that of Wahl's. A few days before Christmas, in 1940—just twenty-one years ago—the cyclotron bombardment was made which, in the succeeding few weeks resulted in the chemical identification of plutonium. Plutonium may be said to have "come of age" as this meeting takes place.

Even at Christmastime in 1940, our work was not done in an atmosphere heavy with historical import, but rather in the carefree manner of young adventurers breaking new ground. It is true that fission and its implications were then known, and that some steps were being taken to learn how to exploit this discovery, using uranium-235. It was theoretically postulated, too, that an isotope of element 94 might be fissionable. Yet there was not, twenty-one years ago, any clear idea of how the then-identified element, if discovered, could be practically made in quantity and how it could be put to use as a military weapon.

Subsequently, with Emilio Segre, we created and identified the fissionable isotope, plutonium-239, in March 1941. And a way was soon visualized to make this element in quantity and to use it as a weapon. In a short time, the knowledge gained in the search for truth became a formidable bulwark of national defense.

We crossed the divide between science and technology, and our work became useful in many ways, including its significant contributions to our arsenal of defense. We went from poverty to relative riches. Instead of working alone or with a colleague or two, we banded together in the team research pattern now so well established.

At times, during the war, we dreamed of a kind of scientific V-Day, after which we would return to the old ways, most especially the pursuit of knowedge for the sake of knowledge alone and divorced from application. Some of you probably were with me in the great hegira to fundamental research which actually did occur at the end of the war.

However, a large number of us found that the conditions of science had changed, in varying ways and to varying degrees. Perhaps the central point is that two decades ago science was called up, as it had been in the Civil War and World War I, to fight a five-alarm blaze. But this time, in a sense, science did not return to the firehouse.

The use of the nuclear bomb crystallized, as never before and on a world stage, the enormous power of science and technology. But this power was not to be confined to war alone, but was to be used for man's benefit in the expansion of industrial productivity and the advancement of our economic system generally. Later in the two decades of which I speak, Sputnik further dramatized the lesson.

Moreover, the realization grew among us and among industrial and political leaders that the time fuse between discovery and application had become short and was growing shorter. The gulf between basic and applied science had narrowed, and in some instances had become imperceptible. This realization was expressed in many ways: for example, while the government after World War II continued the development of nuclear weapons, it dared not risk failure at the same time to support the fundamental research in particle physics. In addition, under the conditions of modern competition between great nations, the prestige and power of a society came to be measured in part by its accomplishments in the growth of all knowledge.

In the past two decades, then, science has come to stay, as a regular, essential and pervasive activity in modern society. The signs that ours has become a scientific society are all around us. Suffice it to say here that Government, business and industry are dependent for survival and expansion not alone on technology, but upon an accelerating growth of knowledge deriving from research that once was sometimes described as "pure." Moreover, it appears that nearly everyone is aware of this fact.

Let me give just one example of these developments, relating to the governmental agency of which I have the honor to be chairman. In 1940, there was no such thing as atomic energy. Today, atomic energy is one of our biggest enterprises. The capital investment of the Atomic Energy Commission is $7.5 billion before depreciation. Its annual budget is $2.5 billion. It is true that approximately 75 per cent of this is devoted to defense activities. Yet, some $600 million per year are also dedicated to peaceful arts—to the development of productive industries for the present and the future, such as power reactors and research on controlled fusion; to the advance of medicine and its application; to the growth of knowledge in many areas of fundamental research; to the export of materials and techniques as a part of our international relations program. In addition, there is the private atomic energy industry, involving nongovernmental expenditures of $50 million annually on development, and with a capital investment of $400 to $500 million. And we can hardly visualize the ultimate potential of this great private industry. And yet, all of this emanated from one discovery in basic research.

The new relationship between society and science is also reflected in the spectacular growth of the numbers of people who are doing research and development or who play supporting roles in these efforts. It is to be seen in the Federal budget for research and development—some $9 billion annually, today, compared with about $400 million in 1940. Even more important are the new attitudes—of society in general toward science, and of scientists toward society.

The former is symbolized by the policies of Government and industry. Recognition by the Government of the need to support research across a broad spectrum was slow and spotty after World War II. The tendency has been—and continues to be to a large extent—to support fashionable or dramatic areas and those that might have some early, foreseeable technological value. Considerable progress was made, however, in the early postwar days as a result of the enlightened policies of the Office of Naval Research and the later policies of the Atomic Energy Commission. The National Science Foundation has significantly expanded the concept of governmental support for broad advances in fundamental knowledge, and I believe this trend will continue and will increasingly embrace the policies of special agencies that support research. Today, about 12 per cent of the Federal funds for research and development are used to support basic research fields. In other words, we can detect a fairly general recognition of the fact that the growth of fundamental knowledge, even though it may not have specific foreseeable application, contributes to the general welfare. Perhaps we can even hope for an appreciation for the more subtle cultural values of basic research.

The enormous impact of the past two decades on the scientific community reflects significant integration of science into society. I do not detect any qualitative change in the spirit of scientific inquiry, fortunately. But it would appear that there is an important alteration in the attitude of scientists about the relationship of their work to the larger social environment. Many of us can recall a fairly general feeling of pride among scientists in the isolation of their work from the practical affairs of men. Indeed, it was not difficult to find resentment at any implication that a piece of research should have more than the remotest connection with application. Now, with the reduction of the time gap between basic and applied research, and with growing general appreciation of the value of knowledge, scientists seem more willing to relate themselves and their work to social objectives.

The material conditions have been modified, too. More and more, scientists find that they are supported adequately, if not opulently, and for sustained programs. Funds are available for "elegant" equipment that saves time and gives greater power to investigators. Money can be obtained for assistants to do detailed work, giving researchers more time for creative effort. The improvements are not uniform, of course. Space to work is still in short supply, especially in our graduate schools; yet, new governmental policies promise some alleviation. And the personal rewards are still relatively less for those who train our scientists and generate much of our knowledge, than for many others in our society who play much less significant roles.

The consolidation of science into society is striking in the field of governmental policy and international relations. The Government has become increasingly dependent upon scientists for advice. This is true not only in the sphere of the administration of Government science, but in a much more comprehensive way. Any evaluation of the future of the economy must embrace scientific and technological knowledge. Decisions in military matters are intimately involved with science and technology. And any commitment of portions of our national resources for science and technology themselves must be decided with the help of men of wide knowledge in these fields.

The entry of scientists into important national advisory capacities is an inevitable concomitant of the events of the last twenty years. I believe it is a healthy and essential development, and I have advocated it for many years. It does not seem to me that the influence of scientists in this respect is greater than it should be; indeed, in the national interest, I believe it must increase.

The question of the place of science in Government touches upon some of the critical questions about the future evolution of a scientific society in a democratic context. Our aim must be to use science to strengthen democracy, not weaken it; to expand the potential fulfillment of the individual, not decrease it. We must avoid any erosion of the broad base of informed participation by the electorate. In the past two decades, our democracy has ingested science, but has not yet digested it—a measure of the infancy of our scientific society. This is not surprising, since our previous experience had not prepared us for anything like the explosion of those twenty years. We must expect the next twenty years to be even more dynamic. Therefore, it is urgent that we accelerate the process of assimilation.

A central problem in assimilation, it seems to me, is the extent to which men, including the otherwise well-educated, fail to identify freedom of scientific inquiry with our political and other freedoms. In the somewhat less complicated world of the eighteenth century, a great thinker like Thomas Jefferson could be all at once a political theorist and practitioner, a philosopher and a scientist. His mind could embrace and integrate a very large part of human knowledge. He had, therefore, a clear appreciation of the broadly humanistic values which are the common heritage of all men who pursue the truth.

But, as knowledge grew and fragmented, the specialties went their separate ways. Science has seemed to walk more apart than other fields, perhaps because the details of scientific truth touch infrequently a community of intellectual experience. Science became a stranger even to many intellectuals.

This estrangement has resulted in the paradox with which we are familiar: as science became more important to society, it apparently became less important in the curricula of liberal education. This fact was noticed as long ago as the last century by Thomas Huxley, who pleaded with contemporaries holding a narrow view of humanism to include a more generous helping of science in liberal education. A cultured, or liberally educated person, Huxley maintained, is one capable of making a criticism of life—of evaluating the environment and making enlightened judgments.

Thirty years ago George Sarton wrote in the same vein in his volume *The History of Science and the New Humanism.* He stated the issue, which remains central for our nascent democratic-scientific society, as follows:

> The main issue does not simply concern humanism but the whole of education from the cradle to the grave. And the real question is: will education include science, or will it exclude it? The intellectual elite is at present divided into two hostile groups—which we might call for short the literary and scientific—who do not speak the same language nor think in the same way. If nothing is done, the gap separating them must necessarily increase, together with the steady and irresistible progress of science. Shall we deliberately widen the gap as the old humanists would have it, or shall we take special pains to reduce it as much as we can?

In our own time, C. P. Snow has eloquently drawn attention to the same problem, in his discourses on the "two cultures."

To summarize the matter, I should like to ask a question paraphrasing Huxley: Who in our times can make an adequate criticism of life without knowledge of the ideals, the methods, and the dynamics of science?

The remedies have been widely discussed: a larger content of science in the lower schools and in the universities and colleges; a wide range of efforts to give the public some appreciation of science; a greater effort by scientists to explain their work in popular terms.

All of these measures are needed. It is necessary to bring about a larger understanding of scientific principles. But in striving toward this goal, it may be even more important to promote a greater consciousness of the common heritage of all who pursue the truth. The philosopher, the social scientist, the artist, the writer, the natural scientist—all are intellectual brothers under the skin. Whether their technique involves the distillation of human experience or the ordering of measurable phenomena into statements of principles, their motivations, the quality of their experiences, and their satisfactions are rooted in a broadly defined humanism.

I am sure intellectuals generally know this to be true. Yet it would appear that it is often far back in the consciousness. I wonder if this fact is not responsible for much of the inability of Snow's two cultures to communicate? I wonder if there is not a common language, deriving from a community of basic ideals and purposes, whatever the details of different bodies of knowledge, that is the foundation for communication? I wonder if the barriers are not superficial, even as language is a superficial obstacle between men who share common bonds?

The achievement of a conscious, working realization of the common heritage of truth-seekers—among scientists as well as other intellectuals—can be significant in the successful evolution of our new kind of society. It should make it clearer that the free and uninhibited pursuit of truth in science is a natural part of the right of free inquiry that is inherent in democracy. It should do much to abolish fruitless discussions over whether we should continue doing science and whether scientists should not withhold scientific truths that may be used destructively. It should give wider acceptance of the inevitable growth of knowledge and of its continual change. It should force us to a greater awareness of the need to prepare for and to cope with the hazards that are a paradoxical by-product of the expansion of knowledge.

It has seemed natural to lay some emphasis on science in this discussion of the society that has developed in the last twenty years. I do not wish to give the impression, however, that I believe this new kind of society is the property of science. We cannot, of course, proceed intelligently without integrating into our thinking and our acting the full range of human wisdom. If you have noticed carefully, I have asked primarily for men generally, and intellectuals in particular, to return science to the fold of humanism. It is unthinkable that a democratic-scientific society could evolve constructively without a wide endowment among its people of art, music, history, literature and social dynamics.

We can hardly discuss the future of the scientific society without relating it to the world struggle and the terrible dilemma confronting man as the result of the development of nuclear weapons.

I am reminded of the reaction of many scientists, including some of us who worked on nuclear weapons, to this dilemma— when it became a reality in 1945. Natural scientists sometimes have been called too optimistic and naïve by social scientists. As a group, they are not lacking in idealism. Perhaps it was natural that many of us, recognizing from close at hand the significance of nuclear weapons, set out to advise the world that nuclear war was out of the question. To us, the data were unequivocal, the conclusions indisputable, and the course of action clear. We felt the world would quickly see this—and, seeing it, do something about it.

The half-life of disillusionment varied from individual to individual. Few have changed their minds about nuclear war. But, many have become more sophisticated, if less idealistic. Much of what has been described as naïveté has rubbed off. But we should remember that idealism, happily, has not been limited to scientists. In the period following World War I, experienced statesmen, imperceptibly influenced by scientists, solemnly signed unrealistic treaties outlawing war. Perhaps sophisticated statesmen, aided by sophisticated scientists in an age of science, may be able to combine realism and idealism.

My own instruction in these matters includes the experience, earlier this year, of being appointed by President Kennedy to head the U.S. delegation to the Fifth Annual Conference of the International Atomic Energy Agency in Vienna. This is an agency established to spread the peaceful uses of atomic energy throughout the world. Its problems, I found, are hardly less difficult than those of the United Nations.

I was impressed with the enormous difficulty of finding common solutions to problems—when the effort had to be made with individuals who seem to speak a different language, not only linguistically, but ideologically, and some of whom appear to possess a deterministic faith that is alien to our humanism.

While I found no basis for arrant optimism, neither did I find reason to stop trying. In the absence of any foreseeable breakthrough in diplomacy, it would appear that the best condition of the world we can hope for is a continuing crisis. In the competition of ideas which will accompany the crisis, the victory may be won by the successful evolution, here, of a society combining science and freedom.

Scientists and engineers can continue, as they have in the past, to make a major contribution in this contest, not only by achievements in the laboratory but also by their participation in exchange programs and international meetings, and other contacts with Iron Curtain nations through the medium of basic research when and if the occasions arise. All of these activities are essential to help keep the channels of communication and understanding open.

I believe each of us, scientist and nonscientist alike, must be aware of the importance of his own effort to the preservation of a libertarian society in the continuing crisis. Each of us needs a sense of responsibility and urgency—for the total of our efforts will be decisive, however remote from combat our work may seem. We must not do too little. We cannot delay. We must have both determination and good intentions; and what is most important—*we must act.* As I have advocated in the past, we must expand and raise the level of education all along the line. We must, especially, search out and cultivate the gifted and creative—for it is these that usually make the great breakthroughs in knowledge and understanding. We must mine every vein of our human resources and exploit our talents in the fullest measure.

The democratic-scientific society has taken root in the past two decades, combining the values of freedom and individual worth with the promise of growing material well-being. Can we preserve it—not only for ourselves, but as a choice for other peoples?

I believe we can and will, partly because of the moral strength of freedom and partly because of the material power of our new society. We cannot be blind to the fact that freedom needs strength and determination as well as a good heart. Generosity has its place in relations between men, but it is, unfortunately, a quality not uniformly respected by all nations in relations between themselves. This is why, for example, we must be prepared to negotiate from a position of unquestioned strength as well as undoubted good faith; and negotiate we must: to turn our back on this most hopeful and sensible solution of the differences between East and West would be as foolish as it could perhaps be fatal. But we must recognize that until all nations can proceed from the same definition of right and truth, international agreements which involve our vital interests must incorporate provision for adequate controls against violations as well as provision recognizing the other's rights. We must be firm when our own security is at stake, as well as fair when another's is. I cannot help but recall, in this vein, that eloquent passage from President Kennedy's Inaugural Address: "Civility is not a sign of weakness, and sincerity is always subject to proof. Let us never negotiate out of fear. But let us never fear to negotiate."

Beyond these principles, my confidence in freedom is based upon a personal faith, originating in my interpretation of human experience, to which one must appeal when scientific data are absent or inconclusive. Many times in history the future has not looked bright. However, the things most feared have not always come to pass. Man's native faith and hope in his own destiny have motivated solutions to awesome problems. History does, we know, repeat itself—both in crises and in their resolution —and so, we must trust it will again.

THE CHALLENGE OF UGLINESS [5]

August Heckscher [6]

"Although scientists are busy charting courses to distant planets," wrote Lorus J. and Margery Milne of the University of New Hampshire, "the earth has never recovered from the discovery of the New World by explorers from the Old." Mr. and Mrs. Milne were referring to man's seeming compulsion to wipe out plants and animals, thus upsetting delicate balances in the natural world. Man's transgression upon the environment affects both the works of his own doing and those of nature. Old buildings, however distinctive, evidently must come down to make way for the faceless boxes currently in vogue. Rows of stately elms or maples must be uprooted to open the path for ribbons of concrete. Stands of flowers along the highway must yield to tawdry billboards proclaiming the medicinal triumph of a new nostrum or picturing the ingredients of America's longest homogenized hotdog. Sentiment over the beauty of the land is in many quarters mildly suspect. Despoliation of the landscape and a sort of architectural frivolity, if not callousness, apparently come under the heading of "progress."

Many organizations have vigorously pleaded for the preservation and restoration of natural wonders in the land. Systematic efforts to combat ugliness in the cities and other communities have, until recently, been less conspicuous. During the spring of 1962, an important conference of leaders in government, architecture, art, and business was held to help "save the face of America from further ugliness." Sponsored by the New York Chapter of the American Institute of Architects, the First Conference on Aesthetic Responsibility met in New York City on April 3 for panel discussions and planning sessions which Richard W. Snibbe, chairman of the design committee, hoped would serve as guides to other groups in the nation.

The principal speaker was August Heckscher, recently appointed as special White House consultant on the arts. In a concise statement, he developed the thesis that a "sort of comeliness" in the environment "is wholly as important as other forms of culture in determining the quality of a society." "The things that are created by men working together, consciously or unconsciously," said Mr. Heckscher, "are the most durable facts about a civilization."

[5] Text furnished by Mr. Heckscher, with permission for this reprint.
[6] For biographical note, see Appendix.

Let me say, first of all, that it is a pleasure to be here, in this company, and concerned with this subject. Since being named by the President, I have received many good wishes and many encouraging expressions of support, not only from individuals but from groups and organizations. I am glad to be able to acknowledge them and to say how much they have meant to me and to others involved in this work. The New York Chapter of the American Institute of Architects has been particularly considerate and cordial. I thank them especially.

Now it seems to me that the Challenge of Ugliness is a good topic to begin on—for in declaring myself against ugliness I am certain to be on safe ground. In denouncing ugliness roundly and resolutely, I am hardly likely to lose any of these new-found friends. And I really don't want to lose them: I am going to need them all as we go forward along a path where troubles and perplexities are bound to accumulate. Indeed, I trust that as the work progresses I may continue to earn your good will.

Having said this, I should perhaps conclude and sit down. But I am constrained to confess that opposition to ugliness is not the whole of my platform—nor is a simple declaration the end of my discourse. I believe that our twentieth-century American society is entering upon a new phase, where the concerns and controversies of the past several decades are going to be muted or supplanted and a whole new range of interests is going to excite the public. Leaving aside the ever-present problems of the cold war, what has been the central preoccupation of our common life? It has been Welfare. It has been the satisfaction of the private desires of the citizenry: the increase in their comforts and the multiplication of their possessions. But there is surely an end of the state more noble and enduring than welfare. The old measures in this field have reached a point beyond debate; new measures may still divide us, but they are destined to take their place, in one form or another, in the anthology of accepted reforms. Meanwhile the people begin to look beyond the acquisition of private possessions and indulgence in personal pleasures.

It is hard to know how to formulate these new and larger interests. I have used elsewhere the phrase "The Public Happiness." I like to think that this in some sense describes the satisfactions men find significant when they reach out beyond the search for security and for material benefits.

The arts and cultural activities form an important part of this realm. The widespread, lively interest in the development of the arts—you can discern it in the press, you can feel it amid the public and even in the Congress—is a symptom of a deep movement in public opinion, one of those transformations in our habits and ways of thinking which, once in a generation or so, create wholly fresh demands and possibilities.

Sometimes this enthusiasm for culture seems a little overwhelming. One fears that where such winds are blowing nice distinctions are going to get lost and the highest standards will prove difficult to maintain. The difference between the excellent and the second-rate, between the genuine and the spurious, between the artist and the amateur, are perhaps now in more danger of becoming blurred than in periods when the arts are neglected.

But the capacity to appreciate and enjoy, and the energy to create, certainly exist in a high degree among us. They may yet bring us out into an age of cultural achievement such as our country has not known before.

Now I would like to maintain today, before this audience, that the maintenance of beauty and fitness in the environment— a sort of comeliness in the world around us—is wholly as important as other forms of culture in determining the quality of a society. The things that are created by men working together, consciously or unconsciously, are the most durable facts about a civilization. They outlast the living generation; they carry forward, to be modified by time and by new men, the body of an age. Where we find that men have built meanly, without common purpose or a sense of the ideal, we can be sure that they lived meanly also—or at the very least that they lived with a disproportionate emphasis on the private sphere of life, neglecting the influences which can make a civilization out of an accumulation of individual existences.

What, after all, do we mean by a civilization? It is surely not the accumulation of private things. Not is it, necessarily, the building of public things. In the *Republic,* Plato complained of those who had heaped up physical structures and yet missed the most important aspects of a true civilization. They have filled the city, Plato complains, "full of harbors and docks and buildings and all that," and have "left no room for temperance or justice." Many of those arguing today that we have over-developed the private sector while neglecting the public sector fall into this fallacy; they seem to suggest that money spent in the public realm is necessarily and in all circumstances a boon.

Granted there are public needs poorly met and some not met at all, still a transfer of funds from the private to the public budget is no assurance of a higher degree of maturity and civilization. A civilization requires "temperance and justice" at the core—an inner sense of values in the light of which decisions are made. It implies an external order of things which are not only beautiful in their own way but correspond to a people's intrinsic sense of what is good.

The next decades will be a period of vast building and of great physical transformations of the American scene. It is not only that goods will pour from the factories. New highways will crisscross the country. Cities will be torn down and rebuilt. The countryside will be made over into new forms of urban and suburban communities. Yet all this activity will not in itself mean that a civilization is being shaped. A civilization begins to manifest itself when men and women have begun to take thought about what it is they construct, and why, and to what end. It begins to be a living whole when the idea of beauty has found its place alongside the pressure of utility and the spur of need.

In the past history of this country, the outward pattern of things has, to an extraordinary degree, been left to chance—to the haphazard actions of special interests and groups. Sometimes it has seemed that as a nation we simply did not concern ourselves with the face of the land. The American continent was so huge, its resources of land and forests and water so unbounded, that though men chopped away at them with only their own interests in mind we trusted that the great bulk of things would remain unspoiled. Sometimes we have assumed that private interests working competitively would create their own kind of fitness.

In strange ways this has often happened. The farming landscape, whether tightly knit in New England or spread across the midwestern miles, has its peculiar beauty. The New York skyline reveals a spirit that no sculpture could have matched. But there are limits beyond which this faith in automatic artistry cannot be pushed. Where these limits are passed over, as in the sprawling roadside slums or the monotonous housing developments, the results have often been appalling. And the public has appeared to stand by helplessly.

Public agencies undertaking to mold the landscape or drastically alter the environment, have most frequently acted with a single interest in mind—to speed up traffic, to stop floods, to put roofs over needy people. All these separate things may be to the good. But the fact that these interventions were the work of lonely enthusiasts, or of bureaucratic experts, suggests that something has been amiss. Where was there a concern for harmony? Where was that sense of the whole which alone can give beauty and meaning to what men accomplish by their common toil?

When we look about us at the natural environment today we are struck by the degree to which it is subject to human designs. No part of it is safe from the bulldozer, from the land speculator, from the engineer and road builder. When Theodore Roosevelt and Governor Pinchot started the conservation movement in 1908, their problem was essentially that of preserving a few key areas, or of instituting practices which allowed natural resources to endure and to reproduce themselves. Since then, the power of man over nature has increased enormously. The great advances in human organization, in science and technology, have literally put into our hands the fate of a vast continental expanse. What we do with it is for us to decide. The forests that sheltered our grandfathers we now shelter and preserve. The land that kept them is now in our keeping. We possess the earth as in no sense could it have been said of any previous generation.

Alas, what we do with it is often discouraging enough. The natural scenery may survive in its grander aspects; the great parks and monuments have been preserved and are appreciated yearly by increasing numbers of citizens. Elsewhere, however, the rash of cities spreads ominously from what were once tight and focused settlements; the roads bring their burden of stretched-out, undefined structures and habitations. These suburbs are strip cities, seen from within, bear out the disturbing impression gained from the sky: too often they are defilements of the natural scene, wasteful desecrators of what have been free space and green land.

On sentimental journeys, on campaigns and outings of a summer season, the Americans show themselves still affectingly aware of the values implicit in a noble environment. If only they could heed as attentively the landscape which surrounds them through the rest of the year! It is one thing, they seem to feel, to retreat into the silence and loneliness of a forest (at least as much silence and loneliness as their ever increasing numbers afford)—but another thing to expect beauty or fitness in their everyday surroundings. They want a national park three thousand miles away; they do not seem to care—or to care enough—if there is no park to which they can motor on a Sunday, or one to which they can walk in their lunch hour. They want the wilderness to be forever wild; but they seem unheeding if the roadsides are forever cluttered with billboards.

Judged by the apparent attitude of too many present-day Americans, there is doubt whether we shall ever be able to extricate ourselves from a descending spiral of ugliness and irrationality. What is required is readiness to undertake on a large scale the kind of public works which are truly *public*—in the sense that they serve the highest interests of the citizenry; and truly *works*—in the sense that they are made to endure and to be judged by future generations. Yet it is this kind of undertaking for which it is often most difficult to muster support among the people. No foreign threat is so intangible but it can evoke a readiness to sacrifice and even a positive enthusiasm for the ordeal. No project, however costly or tenuous its returns, will be seriously challenged by the public if it can be shown that undertaking it will increase our material power. But if it is proposed that something be done by the people for their own delight and for the enhancement of their common life, a dead silence ensues. If someone suggests elegance in a public building, the matter is hushed up as if it were a scandal.

We have been prepared to call on the best architects in the country when it has been a matter of building abroad. The embassies and consulates that have been constructed in various countries over the past decade remind us what the United States

can do—and what government can do—when it sets beauty
and excellence as a goal. The cultural center built by the
nation for the people of West Berlin shows that we are not
unmindful of the value of a setting in which great public
events can be fittingly held. At home, however, the story is
different. We still wait to see accomplished a national cultural
center in Washington. We might well feel impelled to ask, in
regard to our own public buildings, whether we consider ourselves
to be so backward or uncivilized that we cannot enjoy the kind
of beauty which we prepare for others.

We feel impelled to ask such a question—and yet in some
dim way we sense an answer more hopeful than the face of
things might seem to warrant. For there is certainly an influence
taking shape which promises for the America of tomorrow a
more sane appreciation of the true values which make a civilization. The environment can be man's greatest work of art;
and it cannot be that while we strive for excellence and beauty
in specific forms of culture—in painting, in sculpture, in literature, in poetry and music—we shall permanently minimize the
significance of the outward world which surrounds us from our
birth and insensibly makes us what we are.

Yet I would remind you in closing of the other side of the
coin. It would be all too easy to fall from the error of under-
estimating the importance of beauty in the environment to the
opposite error, assuming that environment by itself creates men
and citizens. In *The City in History,* that monumental book
which has just won for Lewis Mumford the National Book
Award, the author has some interesting things to say about the
outward aspect of Athens in the classic age of Pericles and Plato.
The picture we have in our minds, he says, is of a town with "a
marmoreal chastity, a purity and rationality." This did not exist
in fact. If the *polis* existed in this form it was afterwards, in
the third century B.C., when the impetus of the great age had
been spent and men were settling down into an existence no
longer fired by ardor and creativeness.

The Greek mind at the top of its bent possessed, besides its
love of abstract perfection and its strong inner order, "the violent,
tormented and irrational aspects . . . one finds in the tragic
dramatists or in the rude horseplay and barnyard smut one
encounters in Aristophanes." The Greek city reflected all this.

No one has been more scathing than Mr. Mumford in his denunciation of modern ugliness; yet Athens, he reminds us, kept in the period when life was at its highest development a "casual jumble and sprawl." "The visible, tangible city," Mr. Mumford tells us, "was full of imperfections: the disorders of growth, the fermentations and secretions of life, the unburied refuse of outlived forms, not yet decently removed, the relics of rural ways not yet adjusted to the continued ordeals and challenges of urban life." Yet the Acropolis crowned it all, its serene form reaching above the town below, finding completion as part of the landscape of rock and blue sky.

In this tension between the old and new, between the perfection of the isolated form on the hill and the seething city below—between, as it were, earth and sky—Greek life found its moment of fulfillment. When that moment passed, Mr. Mumford tells us, "buildings began to take the place of men."

Let us make sure, as we build for ourselves, that men and their cities prove of equal worth. It is not, after all, only beauty itself, but also the striving for beauty that lifts up men and makes a civilization. We shall strive in our own way, as this second half of the century moves toward its meridian. Who shall say that the striving will not bring its own rewards? Who shall know where the greatest achievement will ultimately lie—within ourselves, or upon the enduring face of the things we have created?

CHRISTIAN ETHICS AND FOREIGN POLICY [7]

John C. Bennett [8]

In a closely knit argument delivered in Washington, D.C., on October 27, 1961, before the thirty-fourth annual conference of the Catholic Association of International Peace, Dr. John C. Bennett tackled some of the thorniest problems confronting modern man. Readers who are familiar with his publications—particularly, *Christianity and Communism Today* and editorial comments in *Christianity and Crisis*—will doubtless hear some familiar echoes in this challenging speech. With his characteristic incisiveness, the dean of the faculty at Union Theological Seminary, and one of the most influential Protestant leaders in America, discussed the concept of Christian ethics and national interest, saying that our thought on it

> should move between two poles. One is the recognition that government is a trustee for the national interest. . . . The other pole is the recognition that no citizen, whether he be Christian or Jew or a man of conscience who adheres to no traditional religion, should make national interest ultimate for himself or for his actions and decisions as a citizen.

Dr. Bennett then examined these relationships in the context of the Communist challenge, the cold war, and coexistence:

> Whenever people say to me: "Give me liberty or give me death" and from these noble words deduce a cold war policy that is likely to lead to a nuclear catastrophe, I say: If such a war should come, liberty will probably not survive, and as for death, it is not only your death that is involved but the death of countless people who never made this choice.

Finally he turned to "the most baffling of all of our problems, the difficulty of finding any way that even makes sense in terms of Christian ethics in the face of the threat of nuclear war." He recalled that during the late summer of 1961 there were pressures "to give moral sanction to the initiation of nuclear war against the Soviet Union if we should be frustrated in the use of conventional weapons at some stage in the defense of West Berlin." But, Dr. Bennett observed, "there is a moral leap from the posture of deterrence to the will to initiate nuclear war at some stage in a conflict, and . . . this moral leap

---

[7] Text furnished by Dr. Bennett. Reprinted by permission of Dr. Bennett and Dr. William V. O'Brien, president of the Catholic Association for International Peace.

[8] For biographical note, see Appendix.

has not been faced or discussed among us." Admitting that it was too late for the churches to do much about the Berlin crisis, Dr. Bennett closed his argument by saying:

> But it is not too late for us to ask what are the Christian resources, Protestant and Catholic, to change the pattern of thought about nuclear war in this country and to prepare us for a wider range of choice in the next crisis and the next.

I shall begin with two religious convictions which underlie all that any of us can say from faith about the ethics that should control foreign policy. The first is the affirmation that God is the Lord of the nation, of all nations. As the prophet known as the Second Isaiah said: "All the nations are as nothing before him, they are accounted by him as less than nothing and emptiness." (40:17) And as Amos said much earlier: "Did I not bring up Israel from the land of Egypt, and the Philistines from Caphtor and the Syrians from Kir?" (9:7) The faith that all of the nations are under the judgment and the providence and the mercy of God is central to biblical religion. Since it is the nation that so easily becomes the ultimate object of loyalty for its citizens, this faith that God transcends the nation is always a warning against national idolatry. And it is national idolatry or the idolatry of a human group or system that is the greatest obstacle to the tolerance and humaneness which are the conditions for decent relations among the nations, conditions which have seldom seemed as remote as in this hour.

Close to this conviction about the transcendence and sovereignty of God is teaching about the persistence of sinful pride and self-centeredness on all levels of human life, not least on the level of high moral achievements and often most of all on the level of national or ideological loyalty. This is a warning against what we might call covert idolatry, not the explicit worship of the nation as God but the assumption that God is always on our side.

As we look at the Communist nations we may well be concerned by the fact that they recognize no god above them and seem to make a god out of the Communist scheme or the Communist goal and, provisionally perhaps, out of the party or the state. But it is our temptation to assume that, because our opponents are atheists, God must be on our side, and to overlook the extent to which communism itself is a judgment upon the sins and failure of the middle-class world, upon the Christian world. The very atheism of communism is a judgment upon the churches which for so long were unconcerned about the victims of the industrial revolution and of early capitalism and which have usually been ornaments of the status quo no matter how unjust it has been. The temptation to turn the cold war into a holy crusade is ever with us and in so far as we yield to it we make impossible the tolerance and humaneness which must yet come into international relations if there is to be a future for mankind.

The question which I find most troublesome—and it is troublesome to me personally as well as to students and others with whom I often discuss it—is this question: how can we relate the high and sensitive ethics of the Bible, the ethic of love and humility which Christians find central in the New Testament to the issues of foreign policy, to all of the problems of power, of deterrence, of conflict that fill every day's newspapers?

At the heart of Christian ethics is emphasis upon dynamic love. This involves caring for all neighbors within reach, for their dignity and their welfare. This involves love for enemies and not merely love for those who love us. This involves self-spending and sacrifice without limits. This involves going to the ends of the earth to serve the neighbor there in so far as it is possible. This involves forgiveness—forgiving seventy times seven. This involves a special caring for those whom the world neglects or exploits or condemns, for the lost sheep concerning whom there is more joy in heaven when it is recovered than over the ninety and nine sheep which were never lost.

How in God's name can we relate such an ethic as this to national policies in the midst of the cold war, policies which Christian citizens may find that they must support, or else recommend other policies which raise the same question in principle even though they may seem more tolerable?

I do not have as good an answer to that question as I should like to have but in a few words my answer is as follows: There is no Christian foreign policy, but Christians under the pressure of their faith must seek policies in the circumstances which are most likely to promote justice and freedom and peace, that have the best chance of enabling neglected people everywhere to be raised to a new level of dignity and opportunity. At any given moment the alternatives that are available may be within very narrow limits and each of them may have repellent elements.

It is always possible for the individual Christian or for Christian groups to say that the alternatives that are open for foreign policy are so bad that the best that can be done is to oppose them all and choose a vocation that involves witness to the love of God by word and deed, often by suffering, which by-passes the immediate political issues. I believe that, whether or not we start with the kind of ethical absolutism which conditions us favorably for such a position, any Christian might actually find himself faced with a choice between such evil and hopeless political alternatives that he might feel compelled to choose this special vocation of nonpolitical witness. My only comment on this position today is that, as things are, most of us have to stay conscientiously related to one of the available political alternatives. Even a nuclear pacifist in the United States has to have in mind a second-best policy for the Government because the United States Government cannot be expected to choose the way of unilateral nuclear disarmament which is what nuclear pacifism implies. It would be psychologically and politically impossible for the Government to choose a policy which would leave the Communist world with a monopoly of the most decisive form of power. I must go on and say that I do not think we ought to permit a monopoly of nuclear power in the Communist world even if it proved to be psychologically and politically possible to do so. The need of power is a given element of which ethics must take account.

1. Christian Ethics and Natural Law

Most Protestants agree with Catholics that in public life it is necessary for Christians to be guided by criteria which they share with non-Christians, criteria that can be defended quite apart from the presuppositions based upon revelation. There is a conception of justice that can be normative for the community as a whole though it is a great error to separate justice or other principles that belong to a common morality from the influence of Christian love. Justice should be thought of as dynamic. The formal principle of giving each person his due is not self-sufficient for what the due of any person is depends upon a moral consensus in the community. Both Aristotle and Augustine accepted the fact of slavery though Augustine traced it to the results of the fall rather than to nature. But today no one believes that slavery is the due of anyone. It is justice modified by love that now recognizes that separate but equal facilities for two different races is not only in most cases a sham but is an organized form of humiliation for the minority race and a source of moral corruption for the dominant race. Here ideas of justice have been raised and this process has been influenced by love. The same thing is true of economic opportunities of all kinds and the interpretation of justice in terms of the need of compensating by the community for the effects of inequalities of condition which undermine genuine equality of opportunity. Now it is very important to say immediately that these changes have not come only because of the influence of love. They have come also because of the pressure of those who have been victims of discrimination and exploitation. A community is indeed fortunate that has within it enough moral sensitivity, enough love so that there are champions of the oppressed among the privileged and so that there is, more broadly, an uneasy conscience, a willingness to accept change in spite of sacrifice of advantages. This makes it possible to avoid an absolute conflict between classes.

I have used justice in the more specialized sense of distributive justice as an illustration of a general way of looking at the relationship between natural law and Christian ethics. Not only the conceptions of justice but the possibilities of justice improve in a society which has felt the influence of the gospel, where love in the sense of charity has touched many hearts and where there is some embodiment of its spirit in institutions and in the general expectations that the community has for itself. I am fearful of sealing off natural law from Christian influences and I agree with Professor Paul Ramsey that much of the moral sensitivity that is expressed in the doctrine of the just war is the effect of Christian love. In general terms the idea of the limitations upon violence which is involved in the conception of the just war can be defended on the basis of natural law but there are forms of awareness and there are impulses that do have their source in Christ that may help to refine the concept and that prepare minds to receive it.

Protestants are fearful of developing a system of natural law that is regarded as parallel to revealed ethics. They see some danger that this will gain independence of Christian love. I note that some Catholics are now emphasizing the primacy of charity in moral theology because they share this same fear or uneasiness about the way a system of casuistry may develop from natural law on its own. Also Protestants are fearful of making into a system the distinction between the highest Christian ethic and what can be expected of the average Christian. This is an old argument between Catholics and Protestants and I can see that Protestants often lose the pinnacles of ethics entirely because all things are leveled down to what is not too inconvenient for the average middle-class family. But the Protestant position intends to have all men under the same commandments and the same judgments with recognition of varying vocational possibilities. There is no reduction of the claims of love for anyone though love must make choices between real alternatives and it must often choose the lesser evil. There is forgiveness for all who in faith repent of the evil in their choices. In Protestant theology there is a tolerated ambiguity as to the meaning of repentance for the necessary evil in the least evil choices and the relationship between such repentance and repentance for the pride and self-centeredness that add to the necessary evil of the choice. Also there should be repentance for the effect of pride and self-centeredness on past decisions which limit the present range of choices.

If this seems to presuppose too much freedom for the individual to alter the course of history, the Protestant would probably answer that he is thinking here not so much of private guilt but the participation by the individual in public guilt; and this suggests an area of ambiguity where Protestants may think that Catholics are neater and clearer in their distinctions but at a price, for the dimension of corporate guilt should not be lost even though it may escape the charts of moral theology. Perhaps this dimension is suggested by the words: "Woe is me! For I am lost; for I am a man of unclean lips, and I dwell in the midst of a people of unclean lips." A modern illustration is the Stuttgart declaration in which Christians in Germany who had least objective responsibility for the crimes of Hitler affirmed their involvement in the guilt of the nation. There is a premature complacency engendered by the tendency to chart in advance some permitted actions which would not be counted grave sins but which would have no mark of charity upon them. This destroys the tension prematurely.

I shall conclude this brief discussion of natural law by saying that Protestants, while they distrust parallel systems of natural law and refuse to introduce them into Christian ethics, do not fail to make use of many of the principles of natural law. This is especially true when they cooperate as they must with non-Christians. Let me give you one illustration of a Protestant theologian who renounces natural law and yet reintroduces it through the back door of his thought. Dietrich Bonhoeffer says that

for pagan government the answer is that there is a providential congruity between the contents of the second table (of the Ten Commandments) and the inherent law of historical life itself. Failure to observe the second table destroys the very life which government is charged with preserving. . . . Does this mean that the state is after all based on natural law? No; for in fact it is a matter here only of the government which does not understand itself but which now is, nevertheless, providentially enabled to acquire the same knowledge, of crucial significance for its task, as is disclosed to the government which does understand itself in the true sense in Jesus Christ. One might, therefore, say that in this case natural law has its foundation in Jesus Christ. [*Ethics*, p305-6]

Bonhoeffer seems to me to admit the reality that is often designated by natural law but he is fearful of allowing this to be regarded as a creation of human reason. He also assumes that the God who is its source is the same God who is known through Jesus Christ for there is no other God. Also, he may share the objections to most of the actual stereotypes of natural law which cause it to be conceived in too static terms and in terms that may suggest too great separation from love. But do we not have here a partial equivalent of natural law without which it is impossible for Christians to relate themselves to the realities of history or to cooperate with non-Christians?

2. Christian Ethics and National Interest

I am never satisfied by the way in which anyone deals with this subject. And I have never been able to arrive at an adequate formulation myself. But here I shall make an attempt. Our thought should move between two poles. One is the recognition that government is a trustee for the national interest. Those who lead the nation can stretch the conception of the national interest so that what is done in the name of national interest can also be supported out of a genuine concern for the welfare of other nations. The interest of a nation has value in itself as long as it is not made supreme; it has to do with the well-being of as many million neighbors as there are in the nation, and the nation as such has its own distinctive contribution to make to humanity.

The other pole is the recognition that no citizen, whether he be Christian or Jew or a man of conscience who adheres to no traditional religion, should make national interest ultimate for himself or for his actions and decisions as a citizen. It is difficult to do justice to both of these poles. There are some considerations which may be helpful in many circumstances.

The first is that a prudent concern for the national interest often has great moral value as a limiting concept. This is something that I have learned from our two American writers who have had most to say on this subject: George Kennan and Hans Morgenthau. A nation that crusades for moral ideas that are not consistent with its long-term interest is likely to throw its weight about far too much, to act as though it knew what was good for every other nation. At this moment of world history, restraint in the use of power is often highly moral even when it is only the restraint of prudence. Morgenthau describes the extreme case when he says: "What is good for the crusading country is by definition good for all mankind, and if the rest of mankind refuses to accept such claims to universal recognition, it must be converted with fire and sword" (*In Defense of National Interest*, p 37). A nation that is controlled by ideology may never limit its goals. A nation guided by a prudent sense of national interest may at least be willing to accept limits. Do not we all hope that the time may come when we can be sure that the Russians will be so busy minding their own business, perhaps using much of their energy driving automobiles around Siberia, that they will be less controlled by the ideological impulse to remake the world?

A second consideration is that the real solidarity of mankind means that we can often act for the sake of mutual interests. The United States can quite sincerely aid India for the sake of the people of India and at the same time for the sake of a common human concern to enable India to find a way forward that is favorable to peace and spiritual freedom in the whole world. Often this emphasis upon mutual interest is better than the emphasis upon sheer generosity for the latter begets cynicism and resentment. There are times for heedless generosity even in the behavior of nations, as for example the efforts of many nations to meet the needs of the people of Chile when they were visited by a most destructive earthquake.

Also, even if a nation is to act in terms of what I have called mutual interests based upon the solidarity of mankind, *the sights of the people have to be lifted.* There must be many people in the nation whose concern and imagination greatly transcend all thought of national interest in their identification with the other nations who may be affected by what is done, if the nation as a whole is to be guided by a broad rather than a narrow view of national interest.

A third consideration is that it is to the interests of a nation for its people to be able to live with their consciences. This leads us away from usual conceptions of national interest altogether but certainly it is involved in matters of faithfulness to commitments to other nations or commitments to the UN. It is also a factor when we face the contrast between the wealth of our nation and the poverty of half of the world. Something like this is suggested by George Kennan when he says: "We should conduct ourselves at all times in such a way as to satisfy our own ideas of morality. But let us do this *as a matter of obligation to ourselves, and not as a matter of obligation to others*" (*Realities of American Foreign Policy,* p 47, italics mine). This contrast cannot finally stand, for our obligation to others must surely be a part of any morality which creates an obligation to ourselves. But it is interesting that one of the leading proponents of the emphasis on national interest here points beyond national interest.

Here I come back to the implications of my second pole: the fact that the citizen should not make national interest ultimate for himself. The relations between people *transcend* the relations between governments. The citizen may also be a churchman, a scientist, an artist or a friend with ties in other countries which are part of his own being as a person. A nation or government should want to encourage these ties, should seek to strengthen the nonpolitical relationships between people across national boundaries. Christian churches as part of their essential nature participate in these nonpolitical relationships. Indeed a Christian is a citizen of two cities and his outlook should never be dominated by his allegiance to the nation. Much may be done by the citizens of one country for the citizens in another country which has nothing to do with national interest so far as intentions are concerned. We should recognize that in meeting major national problems intergovernmental activity is often necessary because of the scale of the problems but this should not make any less important the more personal and more flexible things that can be done across national boundaries by voluntary groups. The great missionary movements express Christian solidarity with other peoples. One of the terrible human losses whenever totalitarian governments are in control of a nation is that all of these personal and voluntary relationships are suspected of having a political purpose and they are restricted or entirely forbidden. In some countries Christian missions have become impossible.

3. *Relationships in the Context of the Cold War*

Many of our ethical problems come to a head when we consider the fact of coexistence between the Communist world and our own.

There are those who say that we should not coexist. I do not know what they really want. But I suppose their real meaning is that we should subordinate the concern to prevent nuclear war to the task of resisting communism, and that it is not enough to contain communism, for we must seek a complete victory in the cold war. Any other purpose or policy seems to them to be a case of "making peace with oppression" and is a betrayal of morality.

To all such people I must say that one element in the moral life is the kind of prudence that seeks to prevent the greater evil and that their view of the cold war will almost certainly lead to hot war and to the nuclear catastrophe which will add to the victims of tyranny scores and perhaps hundreds of millions of new victims of war. Also, I say to them that the institutions of freedom in which they claim to believe so fervently are not likely to survive such a war. The survivors will be too much concerned about order and bread to give much thought to freedom. At least, so it may be. Whenever people say to me: "Give me liberty or give me death" and from these noble words deduce a cold war policy that is likely to lead to a nuclear catastrophe, I say: If such a war should come, liberty will probably not survive, and as for death, it is not only your death that is involved but the death of countless people who never made this choice.

Let me very briefly make two suggestions about the way in which we should think and feel about this deep and dangerous conflict in the world.

a. First, I suggest that we try to distinguish in our minds and even in our hearts between our opposition to communism as a faith and an ideology and a political system on the one hand and our attitude toward those nations in which communism is well established on the other. And here I refer most confidently to the Soviet Union. I also refer to China but I have much less confidence concerning what we should think and do about China except that the isolating of China is the worst possible policy. In the Soviet Union at least we are dealing with a society that has moved beyond the worst elements of the revolution and of the Stalinist terror, with people who have remarkable achievements to their credit, with a generation that is more interested in building the new society in Russia than in world revolution even though there is still a troublesome and highly effective foreign policy designed to promote the ends of international communism; with Communist leaders who have learned at least one thing of vast importance for us, that nuclear war would be a catastrophe for their country as well as for the capitalistic countries to which they are opposed. We should also realize that one element in the feelings of the Russian nation toward us is fear that the United States may at some point in the future attack the Soviet Union. One of the results of our violent hostility to communism is that it would be difficult for people in Russia not to think that, if we ever had a chance, we would destroy communism in Russia. I know that no responsible person in the United States today has any such intention but it would not be strange if the Russians still had this fear. We are opposed to communism as a faith and as an ideology and as a political system, and we will do what we can to keep any Communist nation from imposing communism upon any other nation, but we can still make this distinction between communism as such and the Soviet Union as a nation or China as a nation. What hope we have for the people in the

Soviet Union or in China must be hope for developments within their societies, not hope that we may be able to displace communism in either country by an external attack or by encouraging counterrevolution. We should not be engaged in the Chinese Civil War.

   b. Second, I believe that we should take with full seriousness the fact that Communist power is not primarily military power, that the cold war is not primarily a military conflict. It is true that military power has been used to extend communism, that communism in Eastern Europe is chiefly the result of external pressure with the Red army a continuing factor. But the areas where communism is today the greatest threat are areas where economic and social problems cry for quick solutions and where governments are weak and unstable. Communism is one way of bringing about needed changes—a costly way which we would avoid. The attraction of Communist society in Russia may well be far more important than the persuasiveness of ideology. The power of communism to win devoted followers who help prepare their countries for revolution is the power of an idea and of a promise and not the might of Soviet rockets. The only way in which some nations will be saved from communism is for them to develop alternatives to it. How often must it be said that the failure of the comfortable nations to realize the depth of the neglected social problems of half the world is the chief ally of communism in the cold war? Unless this comes to be understood soon—and very soon—by us our military power and our alliances will be of little avail. I believe that this is understood by President Kennedy and many of his associates but there are many circles in which it is still assumed that the conflict is primarily military and there are many powerful forces that do not know that social revolution is a moral necessity, that it is neither right nor possible to prop up the old order. One of the most appalling aspects of the abortive attempt to stimulate a revolt in Cuba against Castro is that the CIA and other agencies of our government seemed to believe that the Cubans would rally to a standard set up by a conservative group of exiles. The fact that the United States is a status quo nation, fearful of radical change and influenced by a large body of opinion that is still committed to an uncritical capitalistic ideology is one of the greatest obstacles to the success of the free world in upholding its own against communism. The utterly self-defeating character of the intransigent form of conservative anticommunism in this country is amazing to contemplate. As a Protestant I hope that the influence of the Pope's recent encyclical, *Mater et Magistra,* will help to change the American mind at this point.

4. Some Reflections on Christian Ethics and the Nuclear Dilemma.

I turn in conclusion to the most baffling of all of our problems, the difficulty of finding any way that even makes sense in terms of Christian ethics in the face of the threat of nuclear war. I have been gratified to find that there is considerable ferment among Roman Catholic theologians and moralists on this issue. I have not heard anything about it from Catholic bishops but they may yet speak. Of course the Pope has spoken. Among Protestants there has been a noticeable silence on the nuclear dilemma except for the pacifist minority. Roman Catholics in a good sense of the phrase have a vested interest in the idea of the just war and today those who are articulate seek to develop this idea in terms of a limited war in the nuclear age. It is interesting that Catholic moralists who are more inclined than Protestant moralists to hold a "devil theory" of communism are more alert than most Protestants to the moral issues involved in a possible nuclear war against Communist nations.

I agree with those who say that a moral deterioration began with the obliteration bombing of German and Japanese cities in the Second World War. It has seemed ever since that the assumption underlying most attitudes is that there are no moral limits to the damage that we may inflict on the enemy at a distance though some moral scruples would still prevent some acts of cruelty against individuals belonging to the enemy close at hand. We still have some sensitivity about what we do to persons whom we see but against unseen persons at a distance anything is permitted. The technology of weapons and military strategy have supplanted ethics. I do want to report that I have noticed a change in recent months in official circles as is indicated by the desperate effort to move away from strategies of massive retaliation with H bombs to limited military measures with conventional weapons.

There has been a remarkable movement from position to position in what Americans are expected to think about the use of nuclear weapons. First we were quite easily convinced that we should have nuclear weapons as a deterrent because the possession of them would almost certainly prevent the need of using them. Then, when pressed about whether or not we would ever use them to make good on the deterrent, most Americans probably were agreed that they would be used massively against an attacking power. I have never agreed that they should be used against the centers of population in another nation whatever the provocation, but I could hardly deny that their use in this way was probable. Today, because of the strategic exigencies in connection with the defense of West Berlin, there is great pressure upon all of us to give moral sanction to the initiation of nuclear war against the Soviet Union if we should be frustrated in the use of conventional weapons at some stage in the defense of West Berlin. I realize that there are all sorts of contingencies here that it is hard to deal with in ethical terms in advance. There is the inconclusive debate between those who believe that tactical nuclear weapons could be used without necessarily causing an all-out nuclear war. Many argue that we might use small nuclear weapons in the Berlin area and still seek to avoid a holocaust. Yet, in spite of these various refinements of the issue, I believe that there is a moral leap from the posture of deterrence to the will to initiate nuclear war at some stage in a conflict, and that this moral leap has not been faced or discussed among us.

One of the sources of confusion in this context is the effort of some experts to convince the American people that even an all-out nuclear war would not be incompatible with the preservation of the values of our civilization among the survivors. But I think that the illusions of the political realists on this subject are as great as the illusions of many moral idealists about other aspects of political affairs. There has been too much statistical discussion of the number of dead and the number of survivors and too little discussion of the quality of life among the survivors. If one thinks only in such terms, forty or even eighty million dead would not necessarily be the end of our society. But there is an astonishing neglect in all of these calculations of the moral and emotional consequences of a nuclear war, such consequences as the breakdown of community, the necessity of sacrificing freedom to order, the danger of having a barbaric struggle for existence. Walter Lippmann predicts that such a war would result in military dictatorship and that it would be the end of our republic. I appeal from the realist, Herman Kahn, who is chiefly responsible for this nuclear optimism, to the more mature realist, Hans Morgenthau, who rejects all of these optimistic calculations. He says of Kahn's own position: "for the fundamental error in the reasoning to which I'm referring, it seems to me, lies in the assumption that the moral fiber of a civilization has an unlimited capacity to recover from shock." He goes on to say that if his own estimate is correct, "then obviously an all-out nuclear war in defense of Western civilization is a contradiction in terms, an absurdity. I must say that this absurdity may occur, but if it should occur, I would still say that it was an absurdity" (*Commentary*, October 1961, p 281).

It may be argued that to say these things now may cause the Russians to think that we are not firm and that they can get away with actions which might actually bring this absurdity into being. There is a good tactical argument along such lines. But what would be the effect upon the religious and moral thinking of the American people if there were never any discussion of the moral issues at stake in the nuclear dilemma, if they are allowed to think that because of the silence of the Church military strategy is the ultimate court of appeal, that no degree of violence is an atrocity if it is perpetrated by us against a Communist nation? There may be a slight risk that this kind of debate among Americans would tempt the Russians to be more reckless about Berlin but there is a greater risk that, if we allow ourselves to be carried along without criticism by those who think only in strategic terms, we will be unable to prepare to do what may prove to be possible during the next decade to reduce the danger of nuclear war to humanity. If the illusions of the most recent realists are allowed to go unchallenged, we will lack the resolution to find new alternatives, to find new ways to counter the advance of communism where nations are most vulnerable to its attraction, to develop new institutions which may deliver us from the arms race.

What we say here and what is done within our churches may be too late to have much effect on the present crisis. But it is not too late for us to ask what are the Christian resources, Prot-

estant and Catholic, to change the patterns of thought about nuclear war in this country and to prepare us for a wider range of
choice in the next crisis and the next.

One final word about the relation of religion to the conflict
between the Communist and non-Communist worlds. The more
that the religious conflict, that is, the conflict between Christianity and communism, can be distinguished from the international
conflict, the better. The international conflict results in separation
of peoples and in hostility. The conflict between Communists on
the one hand and Christians on the other is compatible with relationships between peoples and with works of love. If there can
develop a structure of coexistence between the nations on both
sides of the conflict, then there will remain a struggle for the
minds and souls of people, but the chief weapon in this struggle
on our side will be witness in word and in life to the truth that
we have seen.

"LET'S LOOK AT THE DOUGHNUT" [9]

R. CONRAD COOPER [10]

In a report entitled *Cybernation: The Silent Conquest,* Donald N. Michael, director of planning and programs of the Peace Research Institute in Washington, D.C., remarked that as long as "we choose to live in a world guided by science and its technology we have no choice but to encourage the development of cybernation." Automation and computers are indeed sobering words at this stage of our industrial evolution. According to Mr. Michael, automatic elevators have displaced 40,000 operators in New York City alone; and 50 statisticians, thanks to computers, were able in 1960 to make the calculations required by 4,100 in 1950. The effects of automation in the mass-production industries have of course been even more staggering. There is a bitter irony in the knowledge that machines are being developed to retrain workers displaced by machines.

A more hopeful view of the effect of automation on our economy came from R. Conrad Cooper, executive vice president in charge of personnel services, United States Steel Corporation, in an address on October 10, 1961, at a Labor-Management Relations Institute held at Evansville College, Evansville, Indiana. Evansville was doubtless a happily chosen place to give this speech. Following the loss of several industries a few years ago, the city entered upon hard days. As George Scullin put it: "Five years ago, Evansville, Indiana, was a quaint old river town with an illustrious past, a desperately ailing present, and little future." Through the vigorous action of many committees, however, old industries were revived, new ones were encouraged to come, and the economic life of the community was generally restored. Mr. Scullin quoted a long-time resident of the city as saying: "We used to get up at dawn because we didn't have automation. Now we have to get up at dawn because we do."

Soft-spoken R. Conrad Cooper is no stranger in the land of public relations. During the long steel strike of some half million workers in late 1959 and early 1960, he was chairman of the industry's four-man negotiating team. The union was represented by David J. McDonald, president of the United Steelworkers of America, whose speech on "A Plan for Prosperity" appeared in REPRESENTATIVE AMERICAN SPEECHES: 1960-1961.

[9] Text furnished by Phelps H. Adams, vice president, public relations, United States Steel Corporation, with permission for this reprint.

[10] For biographical note, see Appendix.

In the 1962 labor contract negotiations between the major steel companies and the United Steelworkers, Mr. Cooper again served as chief negotiator for the companies and Mr. McDonald for the union. On this occasion a settlement satisfactory to both sides was reached well in advance of the expiration date of the previous contract.

It is a distinct pleasure and privilege to be with you here at Evansville College this afternoon and take part in the proceedings of the fourth Labor-Management Relations Institute of Evansville's Future, Inc.

I long have been an appreciative observer of your coordinated efforts for community development and industrial growth, and am happy to see what the determined population of a city can do to reverse an unhappy trend and assure itself of a dynamic and profitable future.

It illustrates what Oliver Wendell Holmes, the New England doctor and poet, meant when he said that the way to live to a ripe old age is to have a constitutional disorder and take good care of it.

Unfortunately, such solid economic accomplishments as yours do not always command the public attention they deserve. The American taste for news sometimes seems to be dominated by Poe's imp of the perverse. It thrives on controversy, on conflict, on difference of opinion, on the sensational exception.

Too often, I fear, it pivots on and exploits failure, rather than success.

Let me illustrate what I mean. In July we put an astronaut into space. For only the second time in the history of our country, man who has lived his years within a few miles, at most, of the earth's surface, broke the bonds of gravity, burst from the envelope of the atmosphere and soared more than one hundred miles into space.

Here was a great effort made possible because of the co-operation of thousands upon thousands of trained and dedicated men—a drama played out against the vast backdrop of the earth, the sea and the sky. The hearts of millions in the audience that followed the flight must have skipped a beat, when, in the critical moments of re-entry, the gravitational pull on the astronaut built above ten G's. For a few seconds, chock-full of suspense, radio contact seemed to be lost. But everything came out all right. The mission was accomplished. Another great adventure was concluded—another vital scientific effort, crowned with success.

And what was the first newspaper headline I saw afterwards. Just two words: CAPSULE SINKS.

Nor is this an isolated instance. There must be something in the mind of man that at times seems to exult at failure. It's an odd thing that every time labor and management meet publicly, the matters that seem to get the most public attention are the points at issue between them, the controversies, the differences.

Very little is heard of those things we have in common, the points on which we agree, the fertile ground that makes industrial growth possible and is our national well-spring of a promising future for prosperity at home and peace in the world.

This is a negative, destructive trend which we need to reverse. It is our duty to minimize man's propensity to dwell on conflict and discord. Let's remember the humorist's definition of the difference between the optimist and the pessimist. Let's look at the doughnut instead of the hole.

Back in January of this year, when the steel companies' negotiating team met with representatives of the Steelworkers Union, I suggested that instead of pinpointing our differences, we try to find something on which we could agree and make that the subject of our public statement.

We did find one area we could agree upon: that the way to create more jobs was to make and sell more steel. Small, perhaps, but it was a beginning. And from now on, when the negotiating teams meet, I am hoping we can find larger areas of agreement on which to base our statements.

That's what I mean when I say, let's look at the doughnut instead of the hole. Let's assess the extent to which labor and management are of one mind. Let's look at the areas on which we agree and on which we can build. That is what you people have been doing and are doing in Evansville. That is what Americans must do all over the country if we are to maintain our place in the world markets and the council of nations.

Too much concentration on the hole instead of the doughnut in our steel negotiations over a twenty-year period resulted in a series of settlements by force that damaged both steel labor and steel management. The consequence was an average rise in total employment cost per man-hour of about 8 per cent per year compounded. During the same period of time, total costs per man-hour rose at about the same rate, but the investment of tremendous sums of money and all other actions to improve productive efficiencies produced an average increase in steel shipments per man-hour of only 2 per cent per year compounded.

The result was a constant and heavy increase in the cost of steel products, which jeopardized the competitive position of our steel products in world markets, and the jobs and employment of steelworkers at home.

This trend we were resolved to stop in 1959, and, although we did not achieve our full objective, we did reduce the annual rate of increase in employment cost during the term of the present agreement by more than 50 per cent.

Still, we were not concentrating entirely on the doughnut. When we do, we will recognize, without reservation, that the interests of the employees and the company are synonymous. They are tied together in economic wedlock, for better or for worse, until death, which, in this case, is the loss of ability to compete, do them part.

When they work together productively and harmoniously, their offspring are more goods, higher profits, more jobs and an abundance of the better things of life for all.

Now, you and I can understand that, to the man out of work, unemployment is a frightening thing. Reason cannot reach him. He is beyond argument in any form. Anyone who has a stake in the economy—and that means everyone—realizes the undesirable social, as well as economic, effect of the empty pay envelope. All of us suffer with the unemployed workers.

The tragedy is, there are some who play upon this fear. They declare, without qualification, that automation is a major cause of the disemployed worker's plight. Machines, they say, are frightful, unfeeling ogres—Frankenstein's monsters that devour jobs.

"Keep your eyes on John Smith," they insist. "Never lose track of John Smith." And, of course, to John Smith, this viewpoint is important. His job is the most important thing John Smith has. And, because he is a human being, John Smith *is* important.

But in addition to John Smith, and as much as we suffer on his behalf, there are other people who must be considered.

What is the positive side?

Certainly John Smith's job is important. But, all too often, because we follow our hearts and keep our eyes focused on John Smith, we overlook Tom, Dick and Harry. They are important—and their jobs are important, too. Still their jobs won't be worth anything if outmoded trends, machines, or methods price—or rather cost—them out of the market. Their jobs—in fact, any job is secure only when it is made efficient and competitive in a profitable business by the best modern tools and procedures available. New methods and machinery will come, in spite of those who oppose them—if not in this country, then in another—if not today, then tomorrow.

Let's look at the doughnut instead of the hole. Man worked his way up from the stone age to our plateau of civilization because he was and is, in Benjamin Franklin's words, "a tool-making animal." "A tool is but the extension of man's hand," said Henry Ward Beecher, "and a machine is but a complex tool. And he that invents a machine augments the power of a man and the well being of mankind."

Through the use of tools, man has built himself a shelter against the elements, reduced the terrors of starvation, moved ahead in the fight to conquer disease, multiplied the number of jobs. Ten years ago, the late Philip Murray said, "I do not know of a single solitary instance when a great technological change has taken place in the United States in the past twenty-five years that has thrown people out of work. . . ." The industrial revolution that has taken place in the United States in the past twenty-five years has brought into the employment field an additional 20 million people.

I am often asked, are we sure of this? How do we know that machines have made more jobs in the United States?

Let me develop the reasoning beyond this as briefly as possible.

Two hundred years ago, which was roughly the start of what we call the industrial revolution, the world's population was about three quarters of a billion. In the next one hundred years it did not quite double. But, from 1860 to 1960, as industry became mechanized beyond the wildest imagination of the inventor of the first steam-driven machinery, the population figure was multiplied four times. Today it approaches three billions.

A transportation system once moved by horsepower in terms of men, horses, donkeys, mules, oxen, camels, and elephants is now horsepower in terms of electricity, missile fuels, petroleum and atoms.

From 1850, when machines did 35 per cent of the work, to the present time, when machines do 99 per cent of the work, the American population grew more than $7\frac{1}{2}$ times. But jobs grew more than $8\frac{1}{2}$ times, and goods and services 34 times. In this period of improving machines and methods, jobs multiplied faster than the population, and goods and services faster than people.

Such growth would have been impossible if we had fought change and thought only in terms of an economy that was 90 per cent agricultural, and 65 per cent dependent on the power of human and animal muscle, as ours was only a little more than one hundred years ago. In 1800, it took nine farmers to feed themselves and one person living in the city. Today's farmer using machines and chemicals produces enough food for himself and twenty-five others.

In spite of this record, workers who permitted themselves to be blinded to everything but the hole in the doughnut, have distrusted and feared machinery. In the eighteenth and nineteenth century workers fought against the introduction of almost every piece of machinery. Their opposition culminated in the Luddite riots of 1811 to 1816, although it was during this very period that England's superior industry was overcoming France's superior military force. Professor Carlton J. H. Hayes has declared, in the era of Napoleon "the ceaseless operation of spinning frames and power looms, of blast furnaces and steam engines, in a country on which the French emperor's army never trod, provided the financial sinews for the military efforts of Britain and her allies and thereby most truly worked his downfall."

We have seen a startling parallel to this in our own times. During the 1930's the game of blaming unemployment on machines started all over again. The refrain of a group of men who called themselves technocrats was that machines permanently displace men. Fantastic suggestions to tax and control machines came from senators and other influential people. Only World War II saved industry from the years of the locust. America became almost overnight, the arsenal of democracy, and produced the tools that worked the downfall of Hitler and Mussolini.

And today, when improved plants and machinery abroad threaten American business, it is only by making our workers more highly productive, through more and better tools and methods, that we will retain our competitive place in world markets.

Some ask, how do machines make more jobs? And I reply, through the good spiral, in contrast to inflation, which is the evil spiral. By making available more goods which consumers want, at the right prices, our standard of living goes up, and Americans generally find themselves wanting and able to secure more goods and services.

The fact that machines make more goods available creates more jobs for others. As the volume of production increases, it takes more workers to sell and market goods. And thus millions of new jobs are opened by growing production demands.

In England, the classic example of this multiplication of jobs came after Richard Arkwright's invention of his cotton-spinning machinery. About 8,000 hand spinners and weavers fought tooth and nail against its introduction. But, in twenty-seven years, textile employment rose more than forty times, to 320,000, and gave Britain one of its greatest industries.

In the United States the classic is the automotive industry. There were 225,000 people making wagons in 1905. Within a few years the automobile had destroyed virtually all of their jobs. But, in their place, thousands of new jobs sprang up. By 1960, more than 2 million were helping to make, sell and service automobiles—ten times the number displaced. How many other jobs opened up—in steel, glass, textiles, aluminum, plastics, wood, rubber, petroleum and metal fabrication—could well be beyond calculation.

Other forms of transportation have grown. Civilians now own nearly 8 million pleasure boats of all kinds. There are 70,000 privately-owned aircraft in the country.

New inventions, such as motion pictures and radio, created thousands of new jobs and opened up new markets. TV didn't sound the death knell of the movies, as had been feared. Radio actually expanded—with 16 million more home sets in 1960 than there were when TV first came on the market. And to top TV and radio, along have come hi-fi and stereophonic.

Despite the competition newspapers receive from television, radio and other news mediums, their circulation has increased by 50 per cent over the last twenty years and their advertising brings in four times the sum it did in 1940.

Telephone calls are in the billions annually, and, with dial telephones nation-wide, more telephone operators are now employed than during the 1920's when the dial system came into extensive use. Spending on travel has doubled in ten years—on books it is up two thirds in six years. We put out $45 billion on leisure activities.

Advances in technology have created whole new industries. In General Electric alone, about one third of the employees work on products that did not exist fifteen years ago.

Through research and market development we are saving old jobs and creating new ones for steelworkers. As a result of long research and development, one of the largest uses of stainless steel is for the bulk handling of milk. After trying other metals, supersonic aircraft are coming back to steel, because of the heat factors beyond Mach 2 and Mach 3. This bears out the 1957 prediction of the Deputy Director of Production of the Air Materiel Command, Brigadier General Clyde H. Mitchell, that within ten years military planes would be 70 to 75 per cent steel.

Thin-tin steel will help us remain competitive with other materials, and help save jobs for steelworkers. Scientists are taking advantage of the strength of steel in Operation Mohole, that underwater attempt to break through the earth's crust. The transportation of desalinized sea water to arid areas of the world will require steel piping in larger amounts. Looking into the future, we may find monorail travel draining the market of steel rails.

Once and for all, we must recognize that we are living in a world of change, not change for the sake of change, but change for the sake of mankind. For decades now we have seen the movement from the farm to the factory. "In every country where they had the chance," wrote C. P. Snow, "the poor have walked off the land into the factories as fast as the factories could take them."

Now we are entering a new phase—a movement out of the factories into the service areas. There are the men who build your television set, and, after you buy it, there are the service men who come into your home, and repair it and replace the burned-out tubes. Advertising in total has grown more than five times in the last twenty years. So have such fields as marketing, research, public relations and my own field of personnel services. In 1949, for the first time, service workers topped the number of production workers.

During the last forty years, a period in which we were engaged in the most rapid and highly developed mechanization in our history, jobs and job opportunities increased by 30 millions.

They were jobs changed in work content—and better jobs. Not only are there now more service jobs than productive jobs, but the quality of all jobs is generally upgraded. The whole complexion of the labor force is getting a face-lifting. White collar workers are increasing in number, and blue collar workers shrinking correspondingly. In this group the greatest spurt of all has been in scientists and technicians.

The reason for this shift, from production to service workers, is easy to understand. Automation is simple mechanization—a better way of doing things. As we produce more goods with less labor we release workers to be used in production of other goods or in services we would not have been able to perform without the new mechanization.

The only predictable fact in this mechanized age—actually, the only predictable fact in all economics—is the fact of change. In the face of this permanence of change no man can remain stationary. No man can expect that his environment will never be transformed, that conditions around him will remain as they are forever. As metals expand and contract with heat and cold, so man must adapt himself to a changing world. We must progress with progress, and grow with growth—and do it intelligently and gracefully.

Professor E. Robert Livernash of the Harvard School of Business put this in a nutshell as far as the steel industry is concerned when he reported, "A major problem confronting the parties in collective bargaining is to adjust to the increasingly competitive environment in a manner best suited to protect their mutual longer-term interests."

The people engaged in our steel negotiations have a twofold responsibility—directly to the plant, company or industry they represent—indirectly to the nation. Closely identified with everything they do is the overriding responsibility that is part and parcel of the people vitally affected.

While meeting and dealing with the economic pressures of industrial life forthrightly, we must handle the human problems in a spirit of the greatest good for the greatest number, with patience, compassion and understanding—especially the latter, remembering the biblical injunction, "With all thy getting get understanding."

These precepts we seek to follow diligently in all our negotiations. Various subcommittees under our human relations research committee have pursued this course in an effort to achieve better understanding of the problems and respective attitudes of the parties in a number of important areas pertinent to the bargaining relationship.

We will do all we possibly can to entertain, encourage and put into practice a cooperative approach to our problems of labor-management negotiations.

We will do this for a number of reasons, recognizing these general facts.

There are ample signs that we live in a period of great world peril—greater perhaps than ever before.

No one can doubt that the ultimate fate of freedom in the world at this moment in history rests primarily upon the United States with its vast economic and military strength.

We all know that this country's economic strength resides in its agricultural and industrial might—developed by courageous people through use of its free enterprise system.

It may well be that the future of our country depends in large part upon the success or failure of collective bargaining, not only as an institution for the handling of employee-employer dealings, but as it affects the economic health of individual plants, companies, industries, and the country at large.

The challenges and great responsibilities thus placed upon employers and their employees, as represented by labor unions of their own choosing, are indeed large, so great and so important in the interest of themselves and their country that they can be met only by cooperation of the highest order. There is no room for conflict. It may be later than we think.

Surely there was never a more important time to look at the doughnut instead of the hole.

PUBLIC ADDRESS AS A SOCIAL FORCE [11]

Ross Scanlan [12]

Some of the distinguished speeches in American history were short: witness, for example, Abraham Lincoln's "Gettysburg Address"; Learned Hand's "The Spirit of Liberty," delivered at an I Am an American Day ceremony in New York, May 21, 1944; and his "A Pledge of Allegiance," given on a similar occasion, May 20, 1945. By and large, however, excellent short speeches are hard to come by. Many are delivered, but relatively few of the texts find their way to the desks of compilers. The reason is clear. Most of the short talks are extemporaneous. If recordings are made, they often suffer the fate of doctoral dissertations by being consigned to inaccessible files.

Ross Scanlan, late professor of speech at the City College of New York, gave the following speech from a manuscript, which was subsequently lost. Fortunately, the talk was taped, and through the kindness of Mrs. Lois C. Golden the text of the transcription was made available for publication.

This was Mr. Scanlan's last speech, delivered on March 11, 1961, at the dedication of new quarters for the Speech Department in Rufus King Hall at Queens College, Flushing, New York. While the printed copy cannot recapture the warmth and eloquence of his superlative delivery, it reveals faithfully the grace of diction, economy of style, and clarity of expression which characterized his public addresses. It reflects, moreover, his dedicated commitment to discussion and debate as instruments for the preservation of democratic institutions. A long-time scholar of the methods of propaganda and mass persuasion in dictatorships, Mr. Scanlan was well-known to students of speech and related disciplines for his essays on "The Nazi Party Speaker System," which appeared in *Speech Monographs* (16:82-97, August 1949, and 17:134-48, June 1950) and *Quarterly Journal of Speech* (37:430-40, December 1951, and 40:1-14, February 1954).

Before an audience like this one, that contains a large number of professors of speech, I think I should apologize for bringing to this occasion what textbooks in our subject condescendingly call a manuscript speech. It has been impressed upon me, both here and at home, that on this occasion brevity has assumed a

---

[11] Reprinted by permission of Mrs. Elizabeth G. Scanlan.
[12] For biographical note, see Appendix.

special importance, and knowing myself, as I think I do, I can think of no better way to ensure brevity than to write what I would like to say and stick to it. So what I have here is not simply a manuscript of a speech; more important for you it is a written guarantee that I will be brief. I hasten to read into the record of these proceedings that it is exactly two and a half pages long, double spaced, and with the appropriate wide margins.

If the past half century has given us any growth in political wisdom, it is, I think, in the somber realization that the world cannot be made safe for democracy. When Woodrow Wilson made that appeal in his war message to Congress, it was received on both sides of the House and by the people at large with the respect and the approval that it deserved. Few at that time questioned the assumption that given total victory in a total war, democracy would be safe. And the victory came, but not the safety. Nor did safety come with victory in the Second World War. And now it would take a high order of optimism indeed to think that victory or safety or, in fact, anything but annihilation will come with the third world war. The record of hot and cold wars and hot and cold revolutions in the last fifty years forces us to the conclusion that the world will never be safe for democracy; that the democratic idea will always have powerful external and internal enemies. But even in the midst of this gloom and doom there is one comforting thought: apparently the world will never be safe for despotism either. The Communist and Fascist institutions that govern portions of the world today are under as great a threat to their existence as is any democracy.

While we are in this vein of revising the aphorisms of the past, we might look at another in this same context: that a house divided against itself cannot stand. Such is the nature of the conflict between authority and freedom, that we may well come to think that the house of the world cannot stand on any basis other than division, that the spirit of authoritarianism will always challenge democracy, and the spirit of freedom will always be around to challenge authoritarianism.

Possibly some of you are wondering what all this has to do with the dedication of a portion of a building which is to be devoted to teaching public address, debate, and the other arts of speech. Of course the answer is that the teaching of public address, discussion, and debate has a close connection with the issue between a democratic and an authoritarian way of life. It is a clear lesson of history that the amount and the kind of instruction given in these arts provides a very sensitive and accurate measure of the amount and condition of freedom in the society.

I think I am right in saying that no building with the purpose of this one was dedicated in imperial Russia under the Czar, or in imperial Germany under the Kaiser. It is true that their successors, Lenin and Hitler, changed the strategy of despotism very drastically. Their systems, every whit as tyrannical as the older ones, had methodically recruited and trained whole armies of speakers. Today, for example, it is reported that a government publication called the *Agitator's Handbook,* which tells the Communist speaker what to say, has the largest circulation of any publication in the Soviet Union. The Nazis in Germany modeled much of their strategy in mass persuasion on Communist techniques as developed in the Soviet Union. Once the fortunes of the party permitted it, little Dr. Goebbels lost no time in preparing a similar handbook for Nazi speakers. These twentieth-century despotisms have appropriated the arts of the public speaker, but their method of training and supervision only emphasizes the fundamental antagonisms between these two ways of life.

What goes on in these classrooms in this building will be a demonstration of the freedom of thought and expression which our society permits, in fact encourages. And, even more important than that, and different from it, it will be an expression of that degree of freedom that the people in our society want. At the same time, what goes on in the classroom when students are speaking will measure very accurately that sense of self-composed responsibility which is necessarily and inevitably a concomitant of a healthy democracy.

THE FRUSTRATION OF OUR TIME [13]

WALTER LIPPMANN [14]

Regular readers of the *Congressional Record* doubtless observed that the text of Walter Lippmann's address before the Women's National Press Club appeared in three places in the issue of January 11, 1962. Hubert Humphrey inserted the text in the record of the Senate; James G. Fulton, in the House record; and Alexander Wiley, under extension of remarks in the Appendix. The triple entry reflects more than routine duplication. It attests to the enthusiastic response which the address received the previous evening, and to the esteem in which the distinguished author and columnist is held. This is an excellent speech, characterized, as is all of Mr. Lippmann's writing, by lucidity, cogency of argument, uncommon insight, and wise political counsel.

At the heart of Mr. Lippmann's address is the belief that a strong Atlantic Community, composed of nations working together closely, can yet save us from the awful peril of our time. The struggle between the two systems in the world will not end "in any foreseeable time." But "I dare to believe that this powerful Western economic community will be able to live safely and without fear in the same world as the Soviet Union, and that the rising power and influence of the Western society will exert a beneficent magnetic attraction upon Eastern Europe."

The dinner meeting took place on the first night of the congressional session. In attendance were many notables, including Vice President Lyndon Johnson, members of the Cabinet, leaders of the House of Representatives and the Senate, and persons attached to the diplomatic corps.

It is an honor, which I greatly appreciate, to be asked to speak on this occasion; it is also a personal kindness. For Congress is about to convene, and that means that there will be many speeches in the months to come. Experience has taught me that it is always a good idea to be able to speak early in the program. By the time Congress has adjourned next summer, adjourned in order to go out and make more speeches in the

---

[13] The text appears in the *Congressional Record*, 87th Congress, 2d session, 108: A89-90, daily edition, January 11, 1962. A fourth printing of the speech appeared in the Appendix of the *Congressional Record* on February 5, 1962 (108:A818-19). Reprinted by permission of Mr. Lippmann.

[14] For biographical note, see Appendix.

constituencies, your bright and eager faces may not be so bright and eager at the prospect of hearing yet another speech. I am happy to catch you while you are still in such robust good health.

When I sat down to prepare this talk, I considered and rejected the idea of delivering a kind of preliminary message on the state of the Union. I remembered that this will soon be done with much more authority by the husband of a former newspaper-woman. So I decided to talk to you tonight about the state of our minds, the state of our nerves, and perhaps even about the state of our souls.

I am moved to do this by a letter I received just before Christmas. It was from a friend of mine who was a great hero in the First World War. He has been an extraordinarily success-ful man since then, and his letter began in this cheerful fashion. "My dear Walter: Another year of frustration, confusion, and compromise is about over."

I know that my friend is not alone in feeling this way and that during the coming session of Congress there will be many who will say what he says and feel as he does. At different times I suppose all of us share his feelings. There is indeed much frustration, much confusion, and—because we live on earth and not in Heaven—there is, of course, much compromise.

I could have written back to my friend, reminding him that in every year of which there is any historical record, there has been much frustration and confusion and compromise. Anyone who thinks he can get away from frustration, confusion, and compromise in politics and diplomacy should make arrangements to get himself reborn into a different world than this one. Or if that is beyond his powers, he should move to some country where there are no newspapers to read.

However, it is certainly true that in our own time we are experiencing a very special frustration and confusion. There is, I believe, a reason for this. Certainly, if we knew the cause, we might feel better, even if we cannot do quickly something drastic to end the difficulty.

The age we are living in is radically new in human experience. During the past fifteen years or so there has occurred a profound revolution in human affairs, and we are the first generation that has lived under these revolutionary new conditions. There has taken place a radical development in the art of war, and this is causing a revolutionary change in the foreign relations of all the nations of the world. The radical development is, of course, the production of nuclear weapons.

As a scientific phenomenon the nuclear age began with the explosion at Los Alamos in 1945. But in world relations the nuclear age really began about ten years later. For during the 1940's the United States was the only nuclear power in the world. But by the middle fifties and in the years following, the Soviet Union has created an armory of nuclear weapons and has built rockets which have made it, for all practical purposes of diplomacy, a nuclear power equal with the United States.

The essential fact about the appearance of two opposed great powers armed with nuclear weapons is that war, which is an ancient habit of mankind, has become mutually destructive. Nuclear war is a way of mutual suicide. The modern weapons are not merely much bigger and more dangerous than any which existed before. They have introduced into the art of warfare a wholly new kind of violence.

Always in the past, war and the threat of war, whether it was aggressive or defensive, were usable instruments. They were usable instruments in the sense that nations could go to war for their national purposes. They could threaten war for diplomatic reasons. Nations could transform themselves from petty states to great powers by means of war. They could enlarge their territory, acquire profitable colonies, change the religion of a vanquished population, all by means of war. War was the instrument with which the social, political and legal systems of large areas were changed. Thus, in the old days before the nuclear age began, war was a usable—however horrible and expensive—instrument of national purpose. The reason for that was that the old wars could be won.

In the prenuclear age, right down through the Second World War, the victorious power was an organized state which could impose its will on the vanquished. We did that with Germany and with Japan. The damage they had suffered, although it was great, was not irreparable as we know from the recovery after World War II of West Germany and Japan and the Soviet Union.

But from a full nuclear war, which might well mean 100 million dead, after the devastation of the great urban centers of the northern hemisphere and the contamination of the earth, the water, and the air, there would be no such recovery as we have seen after the two World Wars of this century.

The damage done would be mutual. There would be no victor. As far in the future as we can see, the ruin would be irreparable. The United States has the nuclear power to reduce Soviet society to a smoldering ruin, leaving the wretched survivors shocked and starving and diseased. In an interchange of nuclear weapons, it is estimated coolly by experts who have studied it, the Soviet Union would kill between 30 and 70 million Americans.

A war of that kind would not be followed by reconstruction, it would not be followed by a Marshall Plan, and by all the constructive things that were done after World War II. A nuclear war would be followed by a savage struggle for existence, as the survivors crawled out of their shelters, and the American Republic would have to be replaced by a stringent military dictatorship, trying to keep some kind of order among the desperate survivors.

To his great credit, President Eisenhower was quick to realize what nuclear war would be. After he and Prime Minister Churchill had studied some of the results of the nuclear tests, President Eisenhower made the historic declaration that there is no longer any alternative to peace.

When President Eisenhower made that statement, no one of us, I think, understood its full significance and consequences. We are now beginning to understand them, and here I venture to say is the root of the frustration and the confusion which torment us. For while nuclear weapons have made war, the old arbiter of human affairs, an impossible action for a rational statesman to contemplate, we do not have any other reliable way of dealing with issues that used to be resolved by war.

It is enormously difficult to make peace. It is intolerably dangerous and useless to make war about the fundamental issues.

That is where our contemporary frustration and confusion originate.

We are confronted with an extraordinarily tantalizing and nerve-wracking dilemma.

For as long a time as we can see into the future, we shall be living between war and peace, between a war that cannot be fought, and a peace that cannot be achieved. The great issues which divide the world cannot be decided by a war that could be won, and they cannot be settled by a treaty that can be negotiated. There, I repeat, is the root of the frustration which our people feel. Our world is divided as it has not been since the religious wars of the seventeenth century and a large part of the globe is in a great upheaval, the like of which has not been known since the end of the Middle Ages. But the power which used to deal with the divisions and conflicts of the past, namely organized war, has become an impossible instrument to use.

President Eisenhower and President Kennedy are the only two American Presidents who ever lived in a world like this one. It is a great puzzle to know how to defend the nation's rights, and how to promote its interests in the nuclear age. There are no clear guidelines of action because there are no precedents for the situation in which we find ourselves. And as statesmen grope their way from one improvisation and accommodation to another, there are masses of people who are frightened, irritated, impatient, frustrated and in search of quick and easy solutions.

The nuclear age is only a few years old. But we have already learned one or two things about how to conduct policy in this age. It was once said of a British admiral in the First World War that if he made a mistake, he could lose the British fleet and with it the whole war in an afternoon. Mr. Khrushchev and Mr. Kennedy are in a similar position today. In a few days or so Mr. Khrushchev can lose the Soviet state and the promise of a Communist economy. He can lose all the work of all his five-year plans, his seven-year plans, and his twenty-year plans. In that same time, Mr. Kennedy can lose the Constitution of the United States, the free enterprise system, and the American way of life and, along with them, all the frontiers, old and new. I don't think I am exaggerating. A full nuclear war would produce by far the biggest convulsion which has ever occurred in recorded history. We cannot understand the realities of the Khrushchev-Kennedy encounter, which has been going on since they met at Vienna last June, unless we remind ourselves again and again of what war has become in the nuclear age.

The poor dears among us who say that they have had enough of all this talking and negotiating and now let us drop the bomb, have no idea of what they are talking about. They do not know what has happened in the past twenty years. They belong to the past, and they have not been able to realize what the present is.

In this present, only a moral idiot with a suicidal mania would press the button for a nuclear war. Yet we have learned that while a nuclear war would be lunacy, it is nevertheless an ever-present possibility. Why? Because, however lunatic it might be to commit suicide, a nation can be provoked and exasperated to the point of lunacy where its nervous system cannot endure inaction, where only violence can relieve its feelings. This is one of the facts of life in the middle of the twentieth century. The nerves of a nation can stand only so much provocation and humiliation, and beyond the tolerable limits, it will plunge into lunacy. This is as much a real fact as is the megaton bomb, and it is a fact which must be given great weight in the calculation of national policy. It is the central fact in the whole diplomatic problem of dealing with the cold war. There is a line of intolerable provocation beyond which reactions become uncontrollable. It is the business of the governments to find out where that line is, and to stay well back of it.

Those who do not understand the nature of war in the nuclear age, those who think that war today is what it was against Mexico or Spain or in the two World Wars, regard the careful attempts of statesmen not to carry the provocation past the tolerable limit as weakness and softness and appeasement. It is not any of these things. It is not softness. It is sanity.

But it leaves us with a task: because we cannot make war, because we cannot achieve peace, we must find some other way of meeting the great issues which confront us. For life will go on, and if the answers of the past do not work, other answers must exist and must be found.

The answer lies, I believe, in the nature of the struggle between our Western society and the Communist society.

It is often said that the struggle which divides the world is for the minds and the souls of men. That is true. As long as there exists a balance of power and of terror, neither side can impose its doctrine and its ideology upon the other. The struggle for the minds of men, moreover, is not, I believe, going to be decided by propaganda. We are not going to convert our adversaries, and they are not going to convert us.

The struggle, furthermore, is not going to be ended in any foreseeable time. At bottom it is a competition between two societies and it resembles more than any other thing in our historical experience the long centuries of conflict between Christendom and Islam. The modern competition between the two societies turns on their respective capacity to become powerful and rich, to become the leaders in science and technology, to see that their people are properly educated and able to operate such a society, to keep their people healthy, and to give them the happiness of knowing that they are able and free to work for their best hopes.

The historic rivalry of the two societies and of the two civilizations which they contain is not going to be decided by what happens on the periphery and in the outposts. It is going to be decided by what goes on in the heart of each of the two societies. The heart of Western civilization lies on the shores of the Atlantic Ocean, and our future depends on what goes on in the Atlantic Community. Will this Community advance? Can the nations which compose it work together? Can it become a great and secure center of power and of wealth, of light and of leading? To work for these ends is to be engaged truly in the great conflict of our age, and to be doing the real work that we are challenged to do. I speak with some hope and confidence tonight. For I believe that in the months to come we shall engage ourselves in the long and complicated, but splendidly constructive, task of bringing together in one liberal and progressive economic community all the trading nations which do not belong to the Communist society.

I dare to believe that this powerful Western economic community will be able to live safely and without fear in the same world as the Soviet Union, and that the rising power and influence of the Western society will exert a beneficent magnetic attraction upon Eastern Europe. This will happen if we approach it in the right way. Jean Monnet, who is the original founder of this movement, has put it the right way.

We cannot build our future [he has said] if we are obsessed with fear of Russia. Let us build our own strength and health not against any-one, but for ourselves so that we will become so strong that no one will dare attack us, and so progressive and prosperous that we set a model for all other peoples, indeed for the Russians themselves.

At the same time the wealth and confidence of the new community will enable the Western society to assist and draw to it the societies of the southern hemisphere, where social and economic change is proceeding rapidly.

You will have seen that I do not agree with those who think that in order to defend ourselves and to survive we must put a stop to the progressive movement which has gone on throughout this century. This movement began in the administration of Theodore Roosevelt. Its purpose was to reform and advance our own social order, and at the same time to recognize that we must live in the world beyond our frontiers. We shall lose all our power to cope with our problems if we allow ourselves to become a stagnant, neurotic, frightened and suspicious people. Let us not punish ourselves by denying ourselves the hope, by depriving ourselves of the oldest American dream, which is that we are making a better society on this earth than has ever been made before.

Is all this conservative? Is all this liberal? Is it all progressive? It is, I say, all of these. There is no irreconcilable contradiction among these noble words. Do not Republicans believe in democracy, and do not Democrats believe in a republic? Such labels may describe political parties in England; they do not describe political attitudes in the United States.

Every truly civilized and enlightened American is conservative and liberal and progressive. A civilized American is conservative in that his deepest loyalty is to the Western heritage of ideas which originated on the shores of the Mediterranean Sea. Because of that loyalty he is the indefatigable defender of our own constitutional doctrine, which is that all power, that all government, that all officials, that all parties, and all majorities are under the law—and that none of them is sovereign and omnipotent.

The civilized American is a liberal because the writing and the administration of the laws should be done with enlightenment and compassion, with tolerance and charity, and with affection.

And the civilized man is progressive because the times change and the social order evolves and new things are invented and changes occur. This conservative who is a liberal is a progressive because he must work and live, he must govern and debate in the world as it is in his own time and as it is going to become.

VALIDITY OF THE EDUCATIONAL PROCESS [15]

HENRY M. WRISTON [16]

In his thoughtful essay "The Individual" in *Goals for Americans,* Dr. Henry M. Wriston, president of the American Assembly—a non-partisan forum conducted by Columbia University—wrote:

> The educative process should never be distorted by the nation's "need" for scientists, or engineers, or doctors, or any other specific profession or skill. Whenever counseling and curriculum stress vocation primarily they underestimate needs just as vital, though not statistically conspicuous. The nation needs philosophers, poets, artists, critics—and a thousand other sorts of people—in numbers which "manpower analyses" can never estimate.

Dr. Wriston questions whether or not certain of our educational practices are likely to produce the sensitive, responsive individuals of whom society stands in need. At a conference sponsored by the Educational Records Bureau and the American Council on Education in New York on October 27, 1961, he reminded educators that some of their practices were not unlike the huckstering and featherbedding of popular disrepute. We should take careful note, he remarked, "of the color of our educational kettle before we compare it to the advertiser's pot." Educational products as well as commercial wares can be sold on the wrong basis. And featherbedding can be found in the curricula of our schools and colleges. "Courses are padded out, and multiplied like the sands of the sea. Parthenogenesis—infertile reproduction—has never been more fully illustrated."

Dr. Wriston pointed to the National Defense Education Act as an instance of the trend to promote training for practical ends. "As the statute is written the defense of the nation rests upon just one thing—mastery of modern techniques. There is nothing about good citizenship, nothing about personal development. Techniques are all that count."

We are all familiar with the fact that too many advertisers are dominated by a single scriptural passage: "Behold, I make all things new"; appropriately enough it is drawn from the Book of Revelations. They constantly and stridently assert that every product is "new." Often it has been in use for donkey's

[15] Text furnished by Dr. Wriston, with permission for this reprint.
[16] For biographical note, see Appendix.

years—and the choice of that as a measure of time was deliberate, for many people have long made asses of themselves by using it. But the older the product the more the advertiser clamors that it is "new."

There is a careful avoidance of outright falsification. The goods are new in the sense that the particular bar of soap which the customer buys—if anyone still uses soap—is not second-hand. But the proclaimed newness too often consists of a new dye to alter the color; heretofore it was white, now it is pink because "pink makes men propose." Or an insignificant ingredient has been added in order to validate the claim to "newness." It is made scientific and mysterious by giving it letters and a number. The inference is that the higher the number, the more combinations had presumably been weighed in the balance and found wanting before perfection was attained. The purpose is to induce people who are tired of the product to keep on using it, trying to discover what is new about it. It seeks to lure nonusers who quit it some time ago to give it a new trial in the hope that it is different in some significant way from the product they discarded.

Trivia in the product, verbally inflated into significant advances, are all based on "research," the modern substitute for magic. Research is an omnibus word that covers anything from counting fingers and toes to asking 1/100 of 1 per cent of housewives how often they brush their teeth and extrapolating the resultant mendacity into authoritative statistics on the dental care exercised by American women.

It is easy to heap deserved scorn upon huckstering techniques. But we should take careful note of the color of our educational kettle before we compare it to the advertiser's pot. The sad fact is that an enormous amount of educational discussion employs the same absurd tricks. What term is more often heard than "research"; it is a word as much abused in our field as in trade. Proposals for programs in education too often rest upon a proclamation that "something new has been added." The new procedure is marketed with all the energy, the skill, and sometimes the deceit of the huckster. Let me concede at once that not *all* this sorry process is dishonest. Often it is simply naïve. The proponents have no sense of history; their research has been too superficial. As they flail away, they do not realize that they are threshing old straw; they raise dust but produce no nourishment.

The state of our art bears yet another striking resemblance to the shoddier advertising techniques which I have, by oblique inference, been criticizing. Some advertising does not attempt to sell its product for its genuine virtues, which are often very real. Soap will get you clean and used often enough will keep you so. Toothpaste will keep teeth in good shape. Hygiene, however, is too seldom mentioned. These products will make you glamorous. They will provide a skin others love to touch; no one has yet had quite the hardihood to suggest his product will lead to having passes made, but someone will soon breach that barrier of taste. These products will keep romance from fading away. They will make your hair shine so that the opposite sex will flock to your side in satisfactorily surplus numbers. Sex is brought into areas where it is irrelevant. Perfectly good products are sold not for what they actually do; they are marketed for everything else but.

Again let us not be too censorious of others so long as we flatter them by imitation. An advertisement I often hear begins by citing statistics as to the number of people who do not possess a high school diploma.. It then offers a *short* (and that word is given great emphasis), *easy* (and that word gets equal stress) means of getting an equivalent certificate "right at home." This program is given the appearance (maybe the substance!) of official endorsement by a charter from the Board of Regents.

What is offered?—a diploma. I have listened carefully and many times. I cannot recall any hint, much less a promise, of an education; the diploma is all that counts. The promise is to cleanse the outside of the cup. (I hope the allusion can still be understood.) Nothing is said of personal growth, nothing of inner satisfaction, nothing, even, of enlarged knowledge or understanding.

There is endless repetition that, on the average, possessors of a diploma make $50,000 more in a lifetime than a non-possessor. It seems, despite the Harvard boys, to make no difference whether it is in Latin or English, on parchment or on paper. The diploma means cash. The economic motivation is primary. Second only to that, social snobbery gets the play. The possession of a diploma will improve your job and thus your social status. Lenin said, "the material life of society is primary," all other aspects of life are secondary, derivative. He

never said it more explicitly than do these diploma merchants.
Like many others who insist they oppose communism, they
embrace its key doctrine.

You will be saying that I have chosen an extreme example.
Its blatant crudity makes an unusually strong case. Beyond
that concession I will not go. For in a vast amount of our educational discussion the same elements appear, muted, disguised,
papered over—but still plainly to be discerned.

Let me cite a concrete case. I was at dinner with a member
of a state board of education, who was serving as chairman
of its committee to see that teachers took advanced work in
order to "stay alive," and to get a salary increase. Present also
was an exceptionally good teacher to whom this form of artificial mental respiration was being applied. During each five
years she was required to accumulate so many "points." Since
she did not live near the state university, she was forced to take
whatever courses were given within commuting distance by the
extension department.

She listed the courses she had taken during the last few
years. I will not repeat them lest I be accused of extravagance.
There is a further reason for reticence; conceivably, in some
circumstances, one or more of them might possibly have had
value for some registrant. But it was agreed by all around the
table—all in educational work—that none of the courses had
any relevance for her professional improvement, or for her personal enrichment. The state was content that she had accumu-
lated the prescribed number of points. Form was all that was
important; substance was of no concern. She had been required
to tithe with mint, anise, and cummin, without regard to the
weightier matters of the law. I may remind you that the verse
from which that passage is drawn begins with an appropriate
phrase, "Woe unto you." The state board member freely con-
ceded that the instance was more nearly typical than unique.
The effective requirement was not education but credits. It
might be argued, feebly, that this exercise was better than none.
But that argument is based upon a concealed major premise—
that the teacher had no inner intellectual interests which would
stir her to personal initiative. But if that major premise is correct, she was dead beyond resuscitation. Then the intellectual
pulmotor was useless.

Sale of an educational product upon the wrong basis sometimes is just as real even when it is not so transparent. The teaching of foreign languages has long been an open scandal. My own instruction consumed fourteen year courses in four languages. It took place over fifty years ago. I had two magnificent teachers, two or three who were adequate, and several scandalously bad. If you will go back just beyond my memory—to 1823—you will find a denunciation of the teaching of foreign language which made my experience seem halcyon. For a long time, then, need for reform was imperative. Whence came the great thrust for improvement of methods, equipment, results. Did it have a deep intrinsic educational purpose? No, it is part of the National Defense Education Act.

Most people know about the appropriation, but few seem to have read the legislation. It is solemnly incorporated in Section 101 of the Act that "the Congress hereby finds and declares that the security of the nation" requires this reform. The law goes on to declare: "The defense of the nation depends upon the mastery of modern techniques developed from complex scientific principles."

That can only be described as an astounding statement. It is cast in the form of an absolute. There is no qualifying word or phrase such as "to some extent," or "among other things." As the statute is written the defense of the nation rests upon just one thing—mastery of modern techniques. There is nothing about good citizenship, nothing about personal development. Techniques are all that count. I have not misunderstood the act. Its purpose is specific: "to insure trained manpower of sufficient quality and quantity to meet the national defense needs of the United States." Even where it refers to needy students, it does not represent an effort to improve them as persons, only to make them more efficient servants of security. Cynics shrug their shoulders. Legislation is not like cigarettes; it is *not* what's up front that counts. Nothing matters but the money that is at the intake end—and no filter, please.

The aims of this educational reform are public and political. Of the growth of the individual, of the beauty and charm of learning, of the validity of the educational process, there is not a word, not even a hint. This is a hard-headed, no nonsense matter of public safety.

It is conspicuous and irrefutable evidence that there was not enough faith in the validity (hence the significance) of the educational process to produce reform upon an adequate scale. The idea of improvement was marketed on a basis that could be more easily sold to the Congress and the public. Institutions must be bribed to get adequate equipment; the significance of knowledge for its own sake must be replaced by a patriotic motive. That statement about patriotism I am forced to withdraw; it was inaccurate. Patriotism is the individual response to public need arising from love of country. No echo of any such hope appears in the finding and declaration of the Congress. The sole motive is the enhancement of a national power position by the multiplication of technical skills. Patriotism does not enter the picture.

Doubtless many proponents of the new program were motivated by genuinely educational objectives. Many good men and true had struggled for years to make head against budget officers who wanted next year's column to look as much like this year's as possible; they had talked themselves hoarse to administrative officers who were without vision or sensitivity. Perhaps desperation led them to catch onto the chariot of national defense; had it not carried the natural sciences to unexampled heights? Now at last the humanities might profit from Federal subsidy. Those who entertained such hopes paid no attention to the intent of Congress.

The language of the act contains no taint of even a remote humanistic interest. It contains no kind word for the literature of other nations, that vast source of understanding their cultures. There is no encouragement for broadening and deepening one's own perceptions through the vicarious experiences which literature provides in such rich abundance. It is language only, capacity for daily practical communication, to which attention is confined. More explicitly, it is the mastery of modern techniques that is vital, not depth of appreciation or understanding.

The law sought to shift interest away from the humanities. The language makes that clear. Section 101 spoke of correcting "as rapidly as possible the existing imbalances . . . which have led to an insufficient proportion of our population educated in science, mathematics, and modern foreign languages and trained in technology." The Congress appears to believe that we have had too many humanists rather than too few.

In order to make the point perfectly clear, contrast the language of the National Defense Education Act with the tone of the Morrill Act of almost exactly one hundred years earlier. In seeking to stimulate work in agriculture and the mechanic arts, Congress specifically enjoined the subsidized institutions not to neglect "scientific and classical studies."

Moreover, the purpose of the Morrill Act was not to enhance the power status of the nation; nor was it social or political. The declared aim was "the liberal and practical education of the industrial classes in the several pursuits and professions in life." It did not overlook the practical value of the studies; equally it did not scorn, as does its modern successor, the liberal side of education, the development of the person for his own more satisfying self-realization. The contrast in tone of the two statutes authorizing Federal subsidies is so striking that it should have been noticed by all who read it, even as they ran.

Even more striking is the contrast between this new support for teaching and the simple, eloquent language of the Northwest Ordinance of 1787: "Religion, morality and knowledge being necessary to good government and the happiness of mankind, schools and the means of education shall forever be encouraged."

The new program, then, was not humanistic at all. The values sought were extrinsic. The inner meaning of the humanities was neglected; the stress was on utility. This statute dealt with citizens only in terms of their utility to their state; no other value was mentioned. This was training for national power purposes. It does not have the blatant crudity of those who called a generation ago for "social engineering," for treating persons as interchangeable parts—like nuts. Nor does it have the candor of the totalitarians. They boldly proclaim that the citizen is trained in order to be a more effective servant of the state. Nevertheless the statute represents a decided shift in the direction of both these groups. The law carries overtones inherited directly from the Technocrats. They also stressed efficiency, not personal worth. This will be obvious if your memories are not so blunted by successive crises that the propositions of the Technocrats have faded from your minds.

Without the candor of the totalitarians, the new law assists students in order to train them specifically to serve the national interest. They are not to be educated either as good citizens nor

for the pursuit of happiness upon which the Declaration of
Independence laid such great stress, outmoded in the new age.
The current emphasis would have been much less dangerous had
it been expressed in clearer tones. Then, at least, the direction
and danger of the drift would have been so explicit as to sound
an alert. Now all the dangers are hidden behind a dollar sign,
apparently the perfect camouflage. If the money is provided,
why worry how, or for what purpose it was voted.

Perhaps the humanities hoped to garner some of the crumbs
that fall from the table of national defense, but that unearned
dividend would be due to wastefulness or inadvertence, it would
not be related to the central purpose of the law. Moreover, if
the humanities cherished this hope—or illusion—it was a silent
surrender of their main bastion. They could never again assert
the innate validity and urgent significance of their own disciplines. They were conceding them a subordinate, a dependent,
status. And they were doing it cynically, saying, in effect, that
as long as we get the money, the end justifies the means. But in
education, of all things, ends and means are inextricably inter-
twined.

I began by complaining that goods were often marketed on
the wrong basis; I now repeat, let us not be self-righteous in
condemning the hucksters as long as we are content to sell ideas
to Congress on the wrong basis.

There are two more points of profound significance here to
which little or no attention has been paid. The first has to do
with the education of public opinion. In a democracy public
opinion is—in the long run—dominant. Our whole educational system, private as well as public, is dependent upon
citizen interest and sense of public values. There has been
bitter complaint that the public is not alert to the seriousness
of our situation. More specifically, bond issues for new schools
are too often voted down in referenda. If public opinion is
directed always to utility—to financial gain, to national defense—
but never to the inner satisfactions of the educative process, to
its intrinsic values, how is public opinion ever to be mobilized
behind a genuinely humanistic approach to education? If we
perpetually sell our product upon the wrong basis, because it
is quicker, it is easier, it gets more money faster, we merely com-
pound the difficulty—inherently great—of making our appeal for

genuine education (as distinguished from training, however valuable) ever more and more difficult for ourselves.

This is not a speculative matter. The evidence is plainly set forth before our eyes. Who believes the Congress would have made funds available for the advance of learning in language, literature, mathematics, science, for the sake of their own intrinsic values without tying it to a practical necessity arising from an immediate national danger? If the language of the Northwest Ordinance had been offered as its "finding and declaration" the Congress would have rejected it.

Even in national terms this is a short-sighted view. For a brief moment one might try to defend, though not very successfully, the shallow thesis of the National Defense Education Act that "the defense of the Nation depends upon the mastery of modern techniques." But in the long run the viability of democracy—the goal we should have in mind—does *not* depend upon an agglomeration of technicians. All the external power in the world will not save democracy from internal decay. The defense of the nation requires experts, but the life of the nation demands much more. It is a wholly unjustified assumption that a well-trained technician, or any other expert, will make a good citizen. Democracy is not the rule of experts. On a specific technical question the experts (if you can get two experts to agree) are more likely to be right than an ordinary citizen. But the more expert a man may be within his own field, the more is he just another common man outside it. This is well illustrated by the political nonsense that has been visited upon us by some of the most famous atomic experts. Contrary to the explicit assertions of the Congress, the future of democracy lies not in a society of technologists, but in the activities of free, self-directed, intelligent, educated people. Technicians can serve the state, it takes broadly sensitive citizens to direct it.

In his farewell address, which is read once a year to empty congressional seats, George Washington made the argument cogently.

It is substantially true that virtue and morality is a necessary spring of popular government. . . . Who that is a sincere friend to it can look with indifference upon attempts to shake the foundation of the fabric? Promote, then, as an object of *primary importance,* institutions for the general diffusion of knowledge. In proportion as the structure of government gives force to public opinion, it is essential that public opinion be enlightened.

Now that through the processes of history public opinion has become really dominant, Congress sells it short. Instead it pleads for and supports the training of technicians—with apparently the full approval of the educational world.

If you doubt the correctness of that judgment, consider the fact that the same Congress renewed the support of the National Defense Education Act, and then with a whoop and a roar defeated support of public education for the purposes set forth in the Northwest Ordinance and Washington's Farewell Address. The majorities against support of general education were as large as those to continue appropriations for the National Defense Education Act. They also gladly voted funds for federally impacted areas. That phrase sounds like some kind of badly developed educational wisdom teeth! But it has closer resemblances to the pork barrel.

Let me say parenthetically that nothing I have said or propose to say is an argument either for or against Federal appropriations for education including those phases mentioned in this bill. That is an important topic, but it is a different one. It should not be confused with what we are discussing—recognition of the validity and significance of the educational process itself.

When education was the possession of an aristocratic minority it was easy to make the appeal for liberal education to the leisure class on intrinsic grounds. Those days are gone. The appeal must now be to a broad spectrum of public opinion. I do not discount the difficulties we face, but if the educational appeal is persistently based upon utility, then utility will become the acid test by which public opinion will judge the program.

Here in New York City this hard-headed, practical approach has influenced the design of schools. One public official has made outcry against esthetics as extravagant and irrelevant. He actually accuses some schools of possessing architectural merit! Well, if we want a factory product, why not produce it in a factory? If public utility of the end product is the criterion, why bother with esthetics? Only if the educative process is valid within itself, only if it is concerned with the development of the individual as an integer is beauty not only relevant, but essential.

It is true that some manufacturing concerns have been able to prove, to the satisfaction of their directors and stockholders, that an attractive environment and attention to esthetic values improves morale and advances productivity. Unfortunately education has not tried very hard to prove that its product can be so improved. If personal development in the widest sense were really thought to be of value, then the esthetics of environment would be seen as vital, not as extravagance. But as long as we want nothing but efficient earners, beauty is an expensive irrelevance.

That it is so regarded is manifested in some of the postwar dormitories that disgrace our university and college campuses. They are little better than educational cell-blocks. They have a bare legal minimum of cubic air space, the minimum of internal light. Of noise suppression they are heedless. I actually experimented by having a colleague drop a pin on the floor above a room in which I was standing. It was clearly audible. Imagine what a radio or a hi-fi—or high heels—would do. In one well-known institution students were not only given no facilities, such as moldings, upon which to hang pictures, they were forbidden to have any pictures at all. The dean explained the decision by saying that they would choose the wrong ones! It never occurred to him that the university had any responsibility for improving their taste. He would abolish—or at least prohibit—bad taste by forbidding it. The place to learn about art, in his view, is in a course—where else?

In the design and construction of many "housing units"— an apt expression—there is no consideration for personal privacy, much less thought of promoting a private life of the mind. In the standardized furniture, bookcases are conspicuously missing or revealingly small. The plain fact is that not only does the curriculum scamp the liberal arts in many institutions, the whole environment, physical and emotional, would go far to prevent the student from acquiring true cultivation by his own efforts.

Nothing but a total, however unconscious, denial of the validity of the educational process would set at naught all we have learned in the last century about environmental influences upon personal growth. Yet the denizens of these academic slum dwellings are taught—in courses of instruction—to be alarmed at the decay of our cities. Huddled together as they are, they learn of the necessity of green belts and more parks. Is it any wonder when educators stress the wrong things that public opinion is misled?

Not only does misdirected emphasis upon the wrong product defeat effective mobilization of public opinion—and in that manner impair the democratic process—the damage to the American ideal is even more serious. We are accused around the world of being materialists; it is an assertion we hotly resent. We can adduce a great deal of evidence to buttress our rebuttal. Nevertheless any candid review of educational discussion, and of educational offerings, makes it painfully clear that we often go far to validate the charge against us. About 20 per cent of the bachelor's degrees given men as they leave college are in business administration, more than in all the sciences and mathematics combined, more than in engineering and vastly more than in the liberal arts. The number of business degrees shows an increase from a little over 3 per cent after the First World War to its present level. The vast preponderance of undergraduate work in this field is in training in gainful skills, not in personal development, or in the virtues of a citizen. The per cent of the four-year course for these degrees given over to professional work has advanced sensationally—sometimes to 70 or 80 per cent. It is hard under these circumstances to make as convincing a case against our materialism as would be desirable.

I am not denouncing business administration, which has a proper place in the educational scheme, though not to this extent —by a wide margin—at the undergraduate level. It does not first stimulate and then rely upon the continuing education of the individual after he has his degree. The cynics leap upon such a statement. They can show statistically—the modern form of revealed truth—that alumni do not, in fact, continue their self-education. But the cynics confuse cause and effect. If you build your program upon the presumption that the student must learn it now or never, the process is not one which will inculcate the habit of self-education. If you stuff the student with data, if independent reading and study are sacrificed to another course in another subject lest there be a gap in his gainful capacity, you have short-circuited the habits that would lead to continued intellectual growth. If you put your energies into getting him ready for his first job, the long run effect is bad. If you call for the formal solution of synthetic problems by imitative processes you do not stimulate independence of mind, flexibility of judgment, readiness to experiment and to accept failure as an inevitable element in the learning process.

I repeat, I am not singling out business administration save as a sample. I have seen engineering taught as a handbook enterprise, with wholly inadequate stress upon principles, almost complete neglect of any genuine higher mathematics, much less with any room left for humane studies. Or take what is often regarded as a cultural subject; I have seen music taught in so commercial a spirit, with so much emphasis on using it to make a living that it was as anticultural as the most crassly materialistic vocational study. Indeed that is what it was.

The materialistic ideal can dominate any field. Some disciplines lend themselves to it more readily than others, but most great disciplines can be perverted. All that is necessary to attain that end is to accentuate the negative and turn to the defensive. That has become our besetting sin; it is exemplified 100 per cent in Section 101 of the National Defense Education Act.

The defensive mood is partly the heritage of the great depression. It is more than a whole generation since its onset; economically we have not only emerged from it, the gloomy forebodings of a mature economy, of an end to growth are now all but forgotten. The cry today is for faster economic growth; government propaganda in the economic field has taken a 180 degree turn. The same men who then denounced growth now demand it—and at a faster pace.

Emotionally, however, the wounds of the great depression have not yet healed. In the matter of unemployment we still accentuate the negative and search for palliatives. For the most part the suggested programs merely deepen the vocational grooves, impair flexibility and retard retraining. Many of the proposals and procedures, far from making the situation better, actually promote unemployment in the long run.

But of all the defensive moods lingering from the depression, education offers the best example. It is easy to denounce featherbedding among labor unions; some of it is utterly scandalous. It is killing the legitimate theatre. But anyone who is irritated by the practice should take a close look at featherbedding in curricula. Courses are padded out, and multiplied like the sands of the sea. Parthenogenesis—infertile reproduction—has never been more fully illustrated.

Many labor unions have limited apprenticeships; some have virtually closed the door against all but the absolute minimum number of new entrants. They want to protect their jobs not by excellence of performance, not by meeting new competition with more efficient work, but negatively, by curbing fresh competition. All kinds of rules, going far beyond the legitimate protection of seniority, have put rigidities into the economic structure that inhibit vigorous growth. Abandonment of such hobbles upon the economy would go much further than feather-bedding to assure adequate security.

We do right to denounce that kind of sabotage of progress. But we should remember always, when we do, that teaching belongs in the front line so far as restrictive practices are concerned. Defensive mechanisms without number have been embalmed into law. It was done, of course, in the name of "standards," which all too often measure intangibles by number, weight and size, none of which can be determined. One striking effect, however, has been to discourage entry of young people into the profession by erecting irrelevant and occasionally outrageous barriers. In the name of professional improvement, requirements have been enacted into statutes that have no such result; indeed, the opposite is more likely.

We have developed an artificial shortage of teachers and made procedures so rigid that reform is needlessly difficult. Lacking the stimulation of adequate competition, protected by all kinds of security arrangements, the lazy, the incompetent, the uninterested were fastened like leeches upon school systems. Even salaries have ceased to reflect teaching skill and capacity so much as years spent or points gained, without reference to performance. For the excitement, the challenge, the competition that gives zest not only to one's employment but to the whole of life, there has been substituted a system of super-security that tends to rob both profession and avocation of those exciting qualities. Many teachers have surmounted all these hurdles and have done superbly. If they had not, our situation would be desperate. Many others, however, are waiting, in the classroom, for their pensions. When looked at closely all these defensive mechanisms are a manifestation of an over-accent upon material things—the precise charge which is leveled against us around the world. Yet we resent the slur without considering how to make it not only wholly untrue, but demonstrably so.

The Soviets boast of their materialism, they proclaim it as the basis of their social, political—and personal—philosophy. We insist, by contrast, that our basic faith is in the unique value and infinite variety of the individual. No respectable economist any longer believes in the "economic man." Motives are vastly complex, and action reflects balancing many impulses, some of them subconscious. The Russians, despite their highly organized dialectic materialism, have had to make practical concessions to the fact that man does not live by bread alone; they have been compelled to appeal to love of country, to historical episodes—to a vast number of nonmaterial motives and springs of action. Sometimes—as during the war—this process went so far as virtually to eclipse, for a time, their basic philosophy.

We have done the reverse. While we have never denied the value of material incentives our historical philosophy has never made them central. They have been one among many; powerful, indeed, but far from dominant. The core of our political and social philosophy has been moral and our achievements have been most conspicuous when that was held in right perspective. A Scotch philosopher summed it up in two sentences: "A man's true significance does not lie in his job, in his service to society, in his citizenship. It lies in being a man—in the inner quality of his own consciousness." If we really have faith in the inner integrity of the educational process we must restore that faith to its central, its dominant, position. Then all the other values which we rightly cherish will be added thereto—heaped up, pressed down and running over.

There was a time when American optimism not only verged upon, it actually became, bumptiousness. Braggadocio was all too current. For a return to the attitude of the braggart I do not plead; but I do urge a renewed accent upon the positive values inherent in our democratic philosophy.

We are in competition with the Soviets—who can doubt it? Let us meet them not on their terms as the National Defense Education Act explicitly proposes to do. It has the fatal defect of being wholly defensive in tone. The only sound defense is to take the offense: let us move forward upon our own terms. This requires education that cultivates the imagination, disciplines the will, enlarges the area of appreciation and deepens its sensitivity, that toughens mental processes. When those things are done, the skills will be more quickly acquired; their refinement will be a lasting enterprise.

Let us not concede to the Soviets, even by inference, the validity of their fundamental materialistic view of the world. Once that concession has been made, their victory is certain. If, on the other hand, we stick to our own way of life, our strengths are sure to prevail.

SCIENCE, LIFE, AND LANDSCAPE [17]

PAUL B. SEARS [18]

Man's relation to the natural world is one of the persistent themes in prose and poetical literature. Since the dawn of history, the land, water, plants, and animals have given man inspiration, satisfaction, and a certain scale of values. "Return to nature" has always been more than an escapist motto. It has meant a renewed association with the abiding principles of life; with the joys and beauties—both quiet and tumultuous—of a world man did not plan, did not make, but is threatening to destroy.

The threat does not stem alone from atomic warheads. The more primitive tools—plows, saws, shovels, small firearms—can do the job. For man is closing in on the remaining unspoiled areas and on many species of plant and animal life. Ours is a "concrete civilization," and there are those who, insensitive to the appeals of nature, are apparently convinced that man can get along well, perhaps even better, without ties to the good earth. If their view prevails; if the remaining wilderness areas disappear and roads are pushed through what Wallace Stegner calls "the last of the silence," we may never again have the opportunity, as Stegner puts it, to be "part of the natural world and competent to belong in it."

For many years prior to his retirement, Dr. Paul B. Sears was chairman of the conservation program at Yale University. A distinguished ecologist, Dr. Sears has been actively concerned with the proper uses of our natural resources, and with man's relationship to an environment that has felt the very considerable impact of modern science. These and related themes provide the context for the accompanying speech.

Believing that the only hope of establishing "an harmonious adjustment between man and the landscape" under the pressure of increasing numbers lies in the "shaping of our cultural values," Dr. Sears remarks:

> A healthy and enduring relationship between man and landscape must come by adjustment to the rules of the game, not by trying to change them. We know better than to try to squelch a volcano or blow back a hurricane. We forget that

[17] Originally published as Occasional Paper 68 of the University of Hawaii. Reprinted by permission of Dr. Sears; Thomas Nickerson, Assistant to the Provost of the University of Hawaii; and Shunzo Sakamaki, president of Alpha of Hawaii Chapter of Phi Beta Kappa.

[18] For biographical note, see Appendix.

the slower and quieter operations of nature are just as relentless. Our only hope of getting along with them is by fitting
our plans, our operations and our values to them. This, in
technical terms, means that we must modify our culture.

From September 1961 until February 1962, Dr. Sears was a Carnegie
visiting professor of botany at the University of Hawaii. He delivered
this lecture at the University on January 16, 1962, under the sponsorship
of the Alpha of Hawaii Chapter of Phi Beta Kappa.

> *"Thou canst not stir a flower*
> *without troubling of a star"*

So sang Francis Thompson, the British poet. Affirming the
unity of the world of nature, his artistic intuition had been clari-
fied by the Darwinian revolution in human thought. For Darwin,
in demonstrating the infinitely long course of evolutionary process, had shown that environment and life, including that of mankind, were inseparable components of a greater whole.

What the plodding, thoughtful Darwin, whose poor scholastic
record would have barred him from a modern graduate school,
had done, was to revive a belief long lost to Western thought.
This belief, implicit in ancient nature-worship, was in the kinship
of man and other living things. And by a curious contradiction,
it had been sacrificed when Abraham substituted the ram for his
beloved son Isaac, affirming his belief in a single just God, ruling
the universe by law, but reserving for man a place aloof from
the rest of nature.

The faiths, Moslem and Christian, which stemmed from this
break with pagan naturalism, merely intensified the sense of
man's apartness and special privilege. Accretions to the simple
teachings of Jesus pictured this world of mortal man as a place of
tears and trial, to be got through somehow in hope of something
much better, in fear of something much worse.

Centuries later the opening up of new continents with seemingly inexhaustible resources did nothing to dampen the belief of
Western culture that nature could be used as man willed. There
was nothing to nurture the ethic long before expressed in Taoist
doctrine of the Orient, that violence toward nature is an evil,
even as violence toward fellow man. Nor was the situation
helped by a break with the insistence of the medieval Church
that economic activities should be subordinate to ethical
considerations.

This break was formalized by Adam Smith in his principle of laissez-faire, which proclaimed that by each serving his own selfish ends, the greatest good for all would ensue. The land and its resources came to be regarded as simple chattels, to be used or used up at the owner's caprice. Even the destruction of feudalism had its effects, for whatever the evils of that system, it was a pattern of obligation in which land, however badly it might be managed, was an object of stewardship.

The impact of Europe upon the Americas was in many ways disastrous. To begin with, agricultural reforms that had begun in the Netherlands had not reached either Great Britain or Spain at the time of colonization. In Virginia and New England, and westward from both, soil was too often regarded as a mere commodity. On the other hand, in the mid-Atlantic states, settled from the Continent, it was properly managed and conserved.

As for Spain, she had failed to preserve the practices of the thrifty and enlightened Moors and in her settlement of the New World was mostly concerned with the search for gold and silver. Only where these were lacking, as in Costa Rica and the Argentine, were farmers seriously colonized.

An additional factor operated in what is now the United States of America. Her founders, desperately fearing the development of a privileged landed class, enacted early legislation that made it all but impossible for land to be retained indefinitely in family ownership. Thus was removed the incentive, so notable even in modern France, for individuals to husband their holdings for the benefit of their descendants.

An Ohio farm in which I have life interest is a case in point. Its ownership cannot be controlled later than twenty-one years after the death of my son. My grandson will be a sturdy character indeed if he resists the temptation to get all he can while the getting is good, regardless of what happens to the land. Incidentally, but significantly, the abstract of title to this land shows that it changed hands not less than twelve times during the first twenty years after the Indians were driven from it. I would gladly right the injustice to them if it were in my power to do so.

Meanwhile I am taking the fullest possible advantage of scientific management to make this farm productive, but receiving far less than an equivalent investment in sound industry would yield.

I must compete with land being opened up to irrigation by government subsidies ranging from $500 to $2,500 an acre in a time of surplus!

But let us return to the role of science as it affects the landscape. This is not by any means a simple matter. We date the official birth of modern science from the work of Sir Francis Bacon, sometime Lord Chancellor to Elizabeth I. This was followed presently by the influence of the agricultural reform that started in the Lowlands. During the late seventeenth and eighteenth centuries land use and management, joined with an amateur interest in science, became respectable, even fashionable in England.

The rapid development of biology, followed by the twin birth of modern chemistry and physiology about the time of the American Revolution, intensified and refined this vogue of interest in agriculture and the land—a trend which has continued to the present day. We now have superbly trained and magnificently equipped researchers in agricultural fields. In such fashion has one of the most ancient and complex of arts been infused with the benefits of modern science. As proof of this, we need cite only the increased level of production which has created the present, if temporary, surplus on North American farms.

Yet the influence of advancing science upon the landscape has been a mixed blessing. Let us examine some of its effects. The humane application of science from the highest motives has reduced the death rate and prolonged the human life-span, without significant effect upon the birth rate. The mathematics of this situation are simple enough. The habitable earth, though vast, is finite in area and variable from place to place in its capacity to sustain populations. Sooner or later the present rate of human increase, which has no precedent in history, must tax both food supply and living space. But long before this can happen, there will be a tragic loss in the freedom of the individual.

The certainty of this rests upon sheer physical principle. For whenever the number of dynamic particles, be they molecules or men, increases within a limited space, the mean free path of each is constricted. Where people are concerned, too great a concentration brings unemployment—more workers than jobs. It also brings the grim alternative of regimentation or disorder. If one takes cities as an example, economic studies such as those of

Joseph Spengler show that after the most favorable size is reached, further growth costs more than it produces. Chambers of Commerce, whose leaders should understand simple accounting, continue to ignore this fact and do all they can to promote what they call "growth." There is a vast difference between growth and health.

But physical principle goes still further. If one increases the energy within a closed system of dynamic particles, pressure is further increased, as we learn from heating a flask of gases. Since the beginning of this century the use of fossil energy in the internal combustion engine has enormously multiplied the activity of human beings. Speed of motion and communication has been multiplied at least a thousand per cent, to say nothing of the resources drawn upon and dissipated in the form of consumer goods, and the stable surface of the landscape which is being altered.

Man, a biological organism, has at length become a major geological force. This was pointed out clearly in a long-neglected book by Samuel Perkins Marsh, *Man and Nature,* first published in 1866. And Marsh, a traveler and observer of wide experience, also noted that many, if not most, of the changes which man had produced on the landscape were such as to lower its capacity to sustain his activities and those of life in general. He had seen, for example, the ruins of former mighty empires in the Mediterranean region, now marked by desolate surroundings. Correctly he saw that this was due to disruption of natural processes rather than climatic changes, as other and later students were to claim. It is well to recall that these tragedies took place long before the day of the bulldozer.

The damage to man's habitat has been intensified as science has led to the increased pressure of numbers and mechanisms. It is not due to the increase in scientific knowledge per se, but rather to the failure to understand and use the entire range of knowledge we have. We use science unscientifically, selecting its applications for immediate convenience and profit, rather than for its true purpose, which is to give us perspective on the system of which we are inevitably a part.

The very results of science with which we are surrounded, not to say smothered, have broken the intimate contact between the urban majority and the patterns of the natural world which control the destiny of mankind. The brilliant achievements, particularly of physical science, have led to a new and dangerous superstition—the faith that technology can preserve us from any scrape we get into. Many view technology as a way of using natural law to defeat its own inexorable operation. We might call this a superstition of the sophisticated urbanite. I doubt if it is shared by the average farm lad, or by those who go down to the sea in ships, for these are daily reminded of the forces of nature.

This widespread fallacy is not to be dispelled by expressions of opinion and warning, no matter how soundly they may be based. Rather we must look at the record, recent and ancient. We have by this time had enough experience with elaborate chains of technology to know that the greater our dependence upon them, the more vulnerable we become to the slightest failure. New York has more than once been thrown into confusion by power failure, and one can easily imagine what would happen to Los Angeles should there be any mischance in the two-hundred-mile pipe line which brings its supply of fresh water.

But let us examine an infinitely longer record, the history of the earth and its inhabitants. The known antiquity of our planet has expanded vastly from Bishop Ussher's modest estimate of 4004 B.C., and even from Lord Kelvin's judgment, based on his knowledge of physics, that the earth was not much more than twenty millions of years old. Today our closest estimates approach five billions of years. This is twice the age of the oldest known fossils, and at least five thousand times the earliest known evidence of mankind.

The lesson is clear. An infinitely long time has been required to fit the earth for man and to develop him into the organism which he is. During that time life and landscape have become bound together, yet it is clear from the record that while man cannot survive without a suitable environment, this environment, the living landscape, can get along very well without man!

During the near-million years of his existence, the human being has changed physically in no important respect. He is first of all fitted by his physical nature and needs to his surroundings and by their ability to sustain him. What has changed is his culture. He has evolved, not by change in bodily form and function, but by developing new ways and new values to sanction them. So that over and above sheer physical bonds he is related to environment by his actions and beliefs.

For his physical survival man requires food and other organic materials, elaborated by green plants using the energy of sunlight. He also requires pure water and air as well as space for wholesome living. Like other animals he needs exercise, recreation and play to maintain reasonable vigor. These needs, as well as all biological experience, suggest that he will have to adjust his numbers to the capacity of his environment, for science knows of no instance in which any organism can increase indefinitely, without coming to terms with physical limitations. If man is an exception, he is truly a remarkable one.

So far as physical survival is involved, food has been the traditional concern, with water, air, and space taken more or less for granted. Even today attempts to estimate the carrying power of the earth deal largely with food. While its production could be increased greatly, there are hordes of people in crowded lands who live at or below a subsistence level, with the hovering threat of famine never far away. Technology, economics, and politics have not yet solved the problem of distribution.

So greatly has our modern life increased the per capita consumption of water for irrigation, industry and domestic use, in the face of increasing numbers of consumers, that adequate water supply has become a political issue, no longer a matter of theory. Although the surgeon-general of the United States has called stream pollution a national disgrace, it still goes on and efforts to clean up our rivers meet with many obstacles. Meanwhile municipalities, states, and even nations struggle for control of adequate water supplies.

One can live longer without food than without water, and longer without water than when deprived of air fit to breathe. Yet precisely where people are most densely settled the air is becoming steadily worse from industrial waste and engine fumes. Our technology is much more concerned with the elaboration of consumer goods than with the protection of what have always been considered free goods—water and air.

Food, water, and air. This leaves space—a more complicated matter, important for both physical and cultural reasons. Primitive hunters sometimes required several square miles per person to provide food enough. Agriculture changed that, and technology still more. Ohio, crowded when fifteen thousand Indians lived there, now has a population nearing ten million. It does not feed them from its own land, though it might do so in a pinch if people became vegetarians. The Megalopolis along the Atlantic seaboard could not possibly feed its own millions.

I have stated the principle governing pressure of numbers on space, with its attendant loss of freedom. Since freedom is itself a cherished cultural value, let us turn to the question of man's cultural needs. These, to a large degree, perhaps almost wholly, are set by the values of his own group.

Life in Hawaii has been enriched by the contribution of its different cultural groups. We need only mention the tradition of exquisite beauty from the Orient, the love of sunshine, music, and water of the Hawaiians. Life here, despite its activity, seems free from the grimness so evident on much of the mainland.

On the mainland some of the Osage and Navajo measure merit by the number of ponies or other livestock, and by the ability to give, rather than to get. Our leading philanthropists generally acquire this latter value late in life, but even so it is good they do for then they have the wealth to dispense.

In spite of differences, however, one common thread seems to me to run through the value systems of all cultures. This is the imperative need for some kind of certainty and confidence. The world as known by any group must somehow be made to hang together, and every culture has its own internal logic directed toward this end. Only by getting inside of any culture, so to speak, is there any hope of understanding it.

Too harsh a judgment has been passed on the early missionaries, I am convinced, for limiting the association of their children with those of the natives. Had they not respected the humanity of the Hawaiians, they would not have been here. But they could not throw off the chilling effects of one of St. Paul's least admirable views on human behavior in the face of a freer, more natural and—who knows—perhaps a more moral one.

Thus each of us finds his certainties in the values cherished by his culture, though outsiders may regard these as superstitions. It is the merit of science to have added a new dimension to our certainty—confidence in the operation of natural law. Our mistake has been to confine this new confidence to the laboratory and industrial plant, to health and agriculture, without seeing that it operates in the broader context of man's impact on the landscape. Here, as truly as in experimental fields the chemist's test tube or bacterial cultures, the stern laws of balance operate.

I listened with respect and attention to the gallant speech of our young President on the State of the Union. While I have a strong sense of the political and economic facts of life, I listened as a biologist and not as one who wished to make capital, pro or con, of his remarks. To do this was not an exhilarating experience, I assure you. For in all of the problems—unemployment, conflicts of interest, delinquency, to name but a few—I could not help sense the relentless and cumulative trend that comes from pressure of humanity on a finite landscape. Andrew Jackson is reported to have said of his population of thirteen million in 1830 that "unemployment, that ancient specter of the human race, is now forever banished." Nothing is clearer than the fact that unemployment, idle hands with too few jobs, is a function of overpopulation quite as much as lack of ingenuity.

Conflicts of interest result and become more acute as the space available to each individual lessens; delinquency and disease are the offspring of crowding. This is not to say that the United States is now overpopulated so far as its ability to support people is concerned. But the pressure of numbers has reached the point where conventional political measures deal mostly with symptoms and are palliative at best. Only by tackling the truly central problem is there hope of serving our belief in the dignity and importance of the individual.

That this involves planning is clear. Planning must be on two fronts—our rate of population increase and our most efficient use of space. Both are extremely delicate matters. Under our system the only hope of solution lies in the development of an informed public opinion of good will. Both science and the historical record agree that the satisfaction of physical and cultural needs involves an harmonious adjustment between man and the landscape. And modern social science has shown that the only hope of such an adjustment lies in the shaping of our cultural values.

This, then, is the problem toward which I have been driving. A healthy and enduring relationship between man and landscape must come by adjustment to the rules of the game, not by trying to change them. We know better than to try to squelch a volcano or blow back a hurricane. We forget that the slower and quieter operations of nature are just as relentless. Our only hope of getting along with them is by fitting our plans, our operations and our values to them. This, in technical terms, means that we must modify our culture.

Every culture has its own momentum, not easily turned aside or altered. Yet cultures do change. And change comes when individuals begin to look at themselves and their surroundings in new ways. For it is profoundly true that the actions of men and societies are governed by the kind of world in which they think they are living. The cynic thinks that every man has his price, the evangelist that every man has an immortal soul. The believer in democracy is sustained by a faith that, given the facts and a choice, the majority will generally make the better decision. Observe the basis of this—*given the facts.*

This goes much deeper than merely posting or proclaiming the facts. It is notorious that people are poisoned because they so often fail to read labels and directions, or swindled because they do not read the fine print on contracts. Facts do no good unless they become part of our thinking and doing apparatus. To affect a culture they must infuse and permeate society itself. They must be like the rain which soaks into the rich absorbent forest floor, not that which falls upon a tin roof.

Quite briefly, we must begin by trying to produce a society that is scientifically literate, without sacrifice of the humane aspects of training and learning. It is true that we are moving slowly in this direction, discussing, organizing committees and lavishing treasure, but remaining vastly confused by our obsession with gadgetry and specialization. We stereotype the scientist according to a pattern set by the graduate schools and, in my judgment, the influence sifts down and corrupts the experience with science at all levels.

To cite a single, but by no means solitary example. When it was suggested to a prominent scientist, commissioned to work with a group trying to improve the teaching of science, that perhaps he ought to get some firsthand experience at teaching undergraduates, he snorted, "I have my graduate students. Don't think I'm going to waste my time on a lot of beginners."

In refreshing, but all too rare, contrast, let me cite the experience of Professor Frank Griffin of Reed College: In 1936-37 he took over a section of mathematics freshmen in the U. S. Grant High School of Portland, Oregon. This section was composed of the least qualified 10 or 12 per cent—twenty-four students who had all had trouble with grade-school arithmetic and were mostly classified as low I.Q.

Starting with easy material which they could understand and which they could see was useful, he tried to draw ideas and working rules from the youngsters themselves. He wrote on the board homework assignments that carried out classroom developments and eleven times during the year (by his report) the youngsters shouted for longer assignments. Before the year was over his group got algebra problems fully as tough as any of the regular algebra classes. Besides this they got a substantial unit on experimental geometry and some simple work on numerical trigonometry and four-place logarithms.

Such pioneering, I am happy to report, is now being brilliantly followed up and the teaching of mathematics is undergoing a revolution. So, I trust, is the secondary school teaching in other sciences. But my concern at this time is not so much with the individual sciences, as with the general pattern or curriculum of all experience with science. Proficiency in any one is good, but if science is to have the impact on our culture which I have outlined, it must convey a balanced picture of the world of nature as we are now able to understand it. To the best of my knowledge this is now being accomplished in some of the small democracies of Western Europe, but scarcely with us.

Science involves both observation and communication. Experience with it should begin with the learning of mother tongue. The world is full of endless interest to the growing child if we encourage and guide his curiosity instead of stifling it. Were only his future enjoyment at stake, he would still deserve the training of his senses as well as his tongue. And as he moves on through the elementary grades he should have, if we cherish our dreams, teachers who are not overburdened hacks, but who have the leisure and talent to give him some measure of personal attention. For good teaching is above all a highly personal affair.

Still thinking of pattern rather than particulars, no doubt various solutions are possible. Until something more tangible turns up, I suggest no less than four years of science in high school and two in college for an understanding of today's world.

I would further suggest that in high school, we begin with the earth and the system of which it is part. There are few satisfactions greater than reading the story of mountains, rocks, rivers, and seas, observing and respecting the forces they represent. Happily this idea is now being put into practice in Pennsylvania, although geology remains a closed book in most places.

Next I would proceed to the study of living things—organisms alive, familiar, and visible to the naked eye, reserving the microscope until it becomes a privilege instead of a penalty. And last, after there is some perspective on the larger whole, seems to me the time for chemistry and physics, for which earlier mathematics, taught as it could be, is proper preparation.

In college, for those who go there, I would be inclined to reverse this order. Taking two years, worked out as a close-knit unit and taught by men and women who believe in it, I would devote the first to a study of time, space, motion, and matter. This combination of physics and chemistry would call for sacrifice of the current idea that the first course should exist to prepare the small percentage of future specialists for the next course ahead.

The second year I would give over to a study of the earth and its inhabitants, again close-knit and building upon the experience of the previous year. Only those who have had the privilege of teaching the natural sciences to groups that understand physical principles will appreciate the resulting satisfactions to all concerned.

In short, the present pick-and-try of requiring a single science never was a very convincing experience, and has failed miserably to produce an educated public that is scientifically literate, with a balanced view of the world of nature. It has long outlived whatever usefulness it had.

I have tried to be as brief and painless as possible in bringing up what the late Sherlock Gass once called "the intolerable subject of education." But our problem is more complex than in the days when the classics formed a basis of common discourse among educated men. The United States Constitution, framed by men who, however they might disagree, could understand each other, is a shining tribute to the effectiveness of that older phase of intellectual history. We are grateful for the fact that these men shared an appreciation of historical process.

Today we must add, not substitute, a similar measure of common understanding of scientific process and perspective. Government with the consent of the governed also implies their participation. Wise decisions can neither be made nor enforced by any other means. More than this, if we are to reshape our culture to insure its permanence, all ranges of talent within it must be drawn upon.

To reorganize life and operation within even that simplest natural unit, the river basin, requires the collaboration of engineer, lawyer, scientist, artisan, politician, and artist, to name but a few. And cooperation is not possible among those who cannot communicate from a basis of common understanding.

Since the role of the engineer is so obvious, we may take him as an illustration. He is generally recruited from one of the highest intelligence brackets in our schools, and severely disciplined in responsibility. While his professional training is being broadened at some of the better schools, it still leaves him in many cases without any background in biology and geology, not to mention esthetics. Even were he so qualified, the manner of his employment seldom gives him freedom to do more than concentrate on his immediate responsibility, leaving to others its broader consequence. Only when he, his employers and co-workers in various fields share the kind of scientific literacy I have in mind—plus a concern for the common welfare that comes from humane education—can we hope for the fullest benefit of engineering talent.

Like engineering, the legal profession has great responsibilities, and possibilities, too, in our neotechnical age. Yet a few years ago, when it was discovered that only about one in seven Yale undergraduates took any more than the minimum science requirements, much of the trouble was traced back to freshmen counselors, most of whom were law students. Their advice was to stay away from science. It may be also that the science requirement itself was not always overappetizing.

I should like to conclude with emphasis on the vital importance of another calling, whose significance is often overlooked —sometimes I fear by those who pursue it. I refer to the artist, whatever his medium of expression may be. It is an old and neglected saying that "I care not who writes the laws of a country, so long as I can sing its songs." Like many aphorisms, this can be read in more than one way.

The simplest rendering would be "Let me alone to do as I wish." I have no quarrel with the utmost freedom of experimentation or self-expression for any artist. Much of the sort of thing that goes on in modern music, poetry, and painting represents intense intellectual effort and technical skill. Jackson Pollock's "Forest Fire" for example I found to be a remarkable abstraction of essentials, but only because he had been thoughtful enough to label it. Otherwise I would merely have found it a curious and interesting bit of brush-weaving. On the other hand I recall the remark of a visiting French architect who said, "The artist concerned to do nothing but express himself is not necessarily a criminal, but he shares that quality with the criminal."

Beyond self-expression, many of our artists do recognize a further obligation. This is to reflect and interpret the current mood and trend. Oscar Jacobson, the Oklahoma painter, revisiting his native Europe during the 1920's saw impending social revolution in the paintings. Ten years later we listened with disbelief to another Oklahoma colleague, back from Switzerland where he had been born, when he said, "There are only two philosophies with any power on the continent today, naziism and communism."

When I see what I take to be the efforts of many artists today to catch and reflect our culture, I am not, nor perhaps am I supposed to be, uplifted. I find a kind of fatalism, a sense of abdication before our new masters, the machines we have ourselves created. There seems to be far more attention to the random paths of molecules and the Principle of Uncertainty than to vitality and resolution through orderly growth into true organic form. Cancer seems to have a charm that healthy tissue does not possess.

Yet our choice is plainly between despair and the struggle to achieve health. I have always thought that to be a truly great artist one must first of all be a truly great person, not wholly the victim of the contemporary scene, but gifted with hope and vision for the future. As the role of science is to minimize the range of uncertainties, so I view the role of the arts as a charge to comprehend, interpret, and dramatize the certainties and their promise.

Where there is no vision the people perish. Science has enormously enlarged our vision, but it will become our common heritage only as it is made manifest by the creative artist. Those triplet daughters of Philosophy—Ethics, Esthetics, and Logic—

must walk hand in hand in the full light of knowledge to
guide us.

* * *

I am indebted to Professor Norris [Ben Norris, Professor of
Art, University of Hawaii], who has given profound thought to
the issues raised concerning art, for comments that may clarify
the situation. Recognizing, as I do also, that the symbolisms of
science, art, and criticism must always be, in a sense, incommen-
surable, he points out that genuine abstract art is a striving for
a new mystique to express the vastly widened horizons of our new
knowledge.

It is interesting to note that the physicist Oppenheimer
believes that even within the field of science itself the various
branches have passed the point of no return so far as any complete intercommunication is concerned. And apropos of my mention of cancer, the late Dr. Alan Gregg in one of his last addresses stated that the only thing to which he could compare the
present unregulated multiplication of mankind was the behavior of cancer cells. Since Dr. Gregg had devoted his life to the
public health work of the Rockefeller Foundation, his humane
compassion admits of no doubt.

But in speaking of the artist as translator and dramatizer of
the scientific view I had in mind simple fundamentals, long
known and capable of simple expression, yet largely ignored.
Because they so obviously affect the future of mankind, it is
my concern that they become more generally appreciated and
woven into contemporary knowledge and values. And for this
task I regard the artist as essential. But this is no one-shot job.
A long time has passed since Goya so clearly symbolized the
horrors of warfare.

A CLOSER LOOK AT THE STARS

ADDRESS BEFORE THE JOINT MEETING OF CONGRESS [1]

John H. Glenn, Jr. [2]

If, as estimated, about 135 million television viewers saw part or all of Lieutenant Colonel John H. Glenn, Jr.'s orbital flight on February 20, 1962, it would seem unnecessary to give introductory comments on his spectacular achievement. Nearly everyone shared vicariously in his experience, took pride in his courage, and applauded his success in becoming the first American to orbit the earth. In one acclaim, the nation endorsed the closing words of President Kennedy's statement upon the completion of the flight: "Some months ago I said that I hoped every American would serve his country. Today Colonel Glenn served his, and we all express our thanks to him."

Colonel Glenn immediately became a hero. The people took this personable astronaut to their heart, not only out of respect to his valor but because he symbolized a national triumph in the competitive struggle for mastery of outer space. Among the many impressive ceremonies in his honor was the joint meeting of Congress on February 26, 1962, to hear his address to the nation. In addition to the senators and representatives, the audience included the Supreme Court, the diplomatic corps, and the Cabinet. This was an unusual occasion. Excepting the highest officers of the United States and foreign countries, relatively few men—perhaps no more than thirty or forty—have been so honored during our history. According to a report in the New York *Times,* the international interest in Colonel Glenn was shown by the appearance at the joint meeting of 97 of a possible 102 foreign heads of mission.

Colonel Glenn's speech was refreshingly informal. Before the eyes and ears of a nation-wide television-radio audience, he singled out members of his family, friends, and colleagues seated in the gallery or on the main floor. Perhaps his introductions did not conform to protocol, but their friendly, spontaneous style delighted the audience.

With patriotic and religious fervor, Colonel Glenn spoke of his experiences on the flight, the importance of team effort, and the need for

[1] The text appears in the *Congressional Record,* 87th Congress, 2d session, 108: 2653-5, daily edition, February 26, 1962. Photostatic copy of the address furnished by Paul G. Dembling, director, office of legislative affairs, National Aeronautics and Space Administration.

[2] For biographical note, see Appendix.

extensive exploration of space. He kept a fine balance between the lighthearted details and the serious theme, emphasizing man's obligation to put the new knowledge to good use.

This was indeed one of those events in which speaker, subject, and audience were completely in tune.

Mr. Speaker, Mr. President, Members of the Congress, I am only too aware of the tremendous honor that is being shown us at this joint meeting of the Congress today. When I think of past meetings that involved heads of state and equally notable persons, I can only say I am most humble to know that you consider our efforts to be in the same class. [Applause.]

This has been a great experience for all of us present and for all Americans, of course, and I am certainly glad to see that pride in our country and its accomplishments is not a thing of the past. [Applause.]

I still get a hard-to-define feeling inside when the flag goes by—and I know that all of you do, too. Today as we rode up Pennsylvania Avenue from the White House and saw the tremendous outpouring of feeling on the part of so many thousands of our people I got this same feeling all over again. Let us hope that none of us ever loses it. [Applause.]

The flight of Friendship 7 on February 20 involved much more than one man in the spacecraft in orbit. [Applause.] I would like to have my parents stand up, please. [Mr. and Mrs. John Glenn, Sr., stood and received the rising applause of the Members.]

My wife's mother and Dr. Castor. [Dr. and Mrs. H. W. Castor stood and received the rising applause of the Members.]

My son and daughter, David and Carolyn. [David and Carolyn Glenn rose and received the rising applause of the Members.]

And the real rock in my family, my wife Annie. [Mrs. John H. Glenn, Jr., rose and received the applause of the Members.]

There are many more people, of course, involved in our flight in Friendship 7; many more things involved, as well as people. There was the vision of Congress that established this national program of space exploration. Beyond that, many thousands of people were involved, civilian contractors and many subcontractors in many different fields; many elements—civilian, civil service and military, all blending their efforts toward a common goal.

To even attempt to give proper credit to all the individuals on this team effort would be impossible. But let me say that I have never seen a more sincere, dedicated, and hard-working group of people in my life. [Applause.]

From the original vision of the Congress to consummation of this orbital flight has been just over three years. This, in itself, states eloquently the case for the hard work and devotion of the entire Mercury team. This has not been just another job. It has been a dedicated labor such as I have not seen before. It has involved a crosscut of American endeavor with many different disciplines cooperating toward a common objective.

Friendship 7 is just a beginning, a successful experiment. It is another plateau in our step-by-step program of increasingly ambitious flights. The earlier flights of Alan Shepard and Gus Grissom were steppingstones toward Friendship 7. My flight in the Friendship 7 spacecraft will, in turn, provide additional information for use in striving toward future flights that some of the other gentlemen you see here will take part in. [Applause.]

Scott Carpenter here, who was my backup on this flight; Walt Schirra, Deke Slayton, and one missing member, who is still on his way back from Australia, where he was on the tracking station, Gordon Cooper. A lot of direction is necessary for a project such as this, and the Director of Project Mercury since its inception has been Dr. Robert Gilruth, who certainly deserves a hand here. [Applause.]

I have been trying to introduce Walt Williams. I do not see him here. There he is up in the corner. [Applause.]

And the Associate Director of Mercury, who was in the unenviable position of being Operational Director. He is a character, no matter how you look at him. He says hold the count-foul, and one thing and another.

With all the experience we have had so far, where does this leave us?

There are the building blocks upon which we shall build much more ambitious and more productive portions of the program.

As was to be expected, not everything worked perfectly on my flight. We may well need to make changes—and these will be tried out on subsequent three-orbit flights, later this year, to be followed by eighteen-orbit, twenty-four-hour missions.

Beyond that, we look forward to Project Gemini—a two-man orbital vehicle with greatly increased capability for advanced experiments. There will be additional rendezvous experiments in space, technical and scientific observations—then, Apollo orbital, circumlunar and finally, lunar landing flights.

What did we learn from the Friendship 7 flight that will help us attain these objectives?

Some specific items have already been covered briefly in the news reports. And I think it is of more than passing interest to all of us that information attained from these flights is readily available to all nations of the world. [Applause.]

The launch itself was conducted openly and with the news media representatives from around the world in attendance. [Applause.] Complete information is released as it is evaluated and validated. This is certainly in sharp contrast with similar programs conducted elsewhere in the world and elevates the peaceful intent of our program. [Applause.]

Data from the Friendship 7 flight is still being analyzed. Certainly, much more information will be added to our storehouse of knowledge.

But these things we know. The Mercury spacecraft and systems design concepts are sound and have now been verified during manned flight. We also proved that man can operate intelligently in space and can adapt rapidly to this new environment.

Zero G or weightlessness—at least for this period of time—appears to be no problem. As a matter of fact, lack of gravity is a rather fascinating thing.

Objects within the cockpit can be parked in midair. For example, at one time during the flight, I was using a hand-held camera. Another system needed attention; so it seemed quite natural to let go of the camera, take care of the other chore in the spacecraft, then reach out, grasp the camera and go back about my business.

It is a real fascinating feeling, needless to say.

There seemed to be little sensation of speed although the craft was traveling at about five miles per second—a speed that I too find difficult to comprehend.

In addition to closely monitoring onboard systems, we were able to make numerous outside observations.

The view from that altitude defies description.

The horizon colors are brilliant and sunsets are spectacular. It is hard to beat a day in which you are permitted the luxury of seeing four sunsets.

I think after all of our talk of space, this morning coming up from Florida on the plane with President Kennedy, we had the opportunity to meet Mrs. Kennedy and Caroline before we took off. I think Caroline really cut us down to size and put us back in the proper position. She looked up, upon being introduced, and said "Where is the monkey?" [Laughter.]

And I did not get a banana pellet on the whole ride.

Our efforts today and what we have done so far are but small building blocks in a huge pyramid to come.

But questions are sometimes raised regarding the immediate payoffs from our efforts. What benefits are we gaining from the money spent? The real benefits we probably cannot even detail. They are probably not even known to man today. But exploration and the pursuit of knowledge have always paid dividends in the long run—usually far greater than anything expected at the outset. [Applause.]

Experimenters with common, green mold, little dreamed what effect their discovery of penicillin would have.

The story has been told of Disraeli, Prime Minister of England at the time, visiting the laboratory of Faraday, one of the early experimenters with basic electrical principles. After viewing various demonstrations of electrical phenomena, Disraeli asked, "But of what possible use is it?" Faraday replied, "Mister Prime Minister, what good is a baby?"

That is the stage of development in our program today—in its infancy. And it indicates a much broader potential impact, of course, than even the discovery of electricity did. We are just probing the surface of the greatest advancements in man's knowledge of his surroundings that has ever been made, I feel. There are benefits to science across the board. Any major effort such as this results in research by so many different specialties that it is hard to even envision the benefits that will accrue in many fields.

Knowledge begets knowledge. The more I see, the more impressed I am—not with how much we know—but with how tremendous the areas are that are as yet unexplored.

Exploration, knowledge, and achievement are good only insofar as we apply them to our future actions. Progress never stops. We are now on the verge of a new era, I feel.

Today, I know that I seem to be standing alone on this great platform—just as I seemed to be alone in the cockpit of the Friendship 7 spacecraft. But I am not. There were with me then —and with me now—thousands of Americans and many hundreds of citizens of many countries around the world who contributed to this truly international undertaking voluntarily and in a spirit of cooperation and understanding.

On behalf of all of those people, I would like to express my and their heartfelt thanks for the honors you have bestowed upon us here today.

We are all proud to have been privileged to be part of this effort, to represent our country as we have. As our knowledge of the universe in which we live increases, may God grant us the wisdom and guidance to use it wisely.

APPENDIX

BIOGRAPHICAL NOTES

BENNETT, JOHN C. (1902-). Born, Kingston, Ontario, Canada (parents United States citizens); student, Phillips Exeter Academy, 1918-20; A.B., Williams College, 1924; B.A., Oxford University, 1926; M.A., 1930; B.D., *magna cum laude,* Union Theological Seminary, 1927; S.T.M., 1929; D.D., Church Divinity School of the Pacific, 1940; Pacific School of Religion, 1943; Williams College, 1947; instructor in theology, Union Theological Seminary, 1930-31; assistant professor of Christian theology, Auburn Theological Seminary, 1931-35; associate professor, 1935-38; professor of Christian theology and philosophy of religion, Pacific School of Religion, 1938-43; professor of Christian theology and ethics, Union Theological Seminary, 1943- ; dean of faculty, 1955- ; Reinhold Niebuhr professor of social ethics, 1960- ; ordained to ministry, Congregational Church, 1939; foundation lecturer at Chicago Theological seminary, Yale University, Grinnell College, University of Virginia, Garrett Biblical Institute, and elsewhere; Phi Beta Kappa; author, *Social Salvation,* 1935; *Christianity and Our World,* 1936; *Christian Realism,* 1941; *Christian Ethics and Social Policy,* 1946; *The Christian As Citizen,* 1955; *Christians and the State,* 1958; *Christianity and Communism Today,* 1960; co-author, *Christian Values and Economic Life,* 1954; editor, *Nuclear Weapons and the Conflict of Conscience,* 1962; cochairman, editorial board, *Christianity and Crisis;* vice-chairman, Liberal party of New York. (See also *Current Biography: 1961.*)

COOPER, RICHARD CONRAD (1903-). Born, Beaver Dam, Kentucky; B.S., University of Minnesota, 1926; field engineer, service department, Universal Portland Cement Company, 1926-29; consulting engineer in New York, 1929-37; assistant to the vice president of operations, Wheeling Steel Corporation, 1937-40; assistant vice president, 1940-45; assistant vice president, industrial relations, Delaware Corporation, 1948-51; following mergers, vice president, industrial engineering, United States Steel Company, 1951-53; vice president, industrial engineering, United States

Steel Corporation, 1953-55; vice president, administration planning, 1955-58; executive vice president, personnel services, 1958- . (See also *Current Biography: 1960.*)

GLENN, JOHN HERSCHEL, JR. (1921-). Born, Cambridge, Ohio; grew up in New Concord, Ohio; entered Muskingum College, 1939; left in junior year to join Navy preflight program; honorary D.Sc., Muskingum College, 1961; joined Marine Corps, 1943; combat pilot in World War II and Korean War; set transcontinental flight record of 3 hours 23 minutes, 1957; first American to make orbital flight, February 20, 1962; holder of five Distinguished Flying Crosses; Air Medal with 18 clusters; NASA Distinguished Service Medal. (See also *Current Biography: June 1962.*)

HECKSCHER, AUGUST (1913-). Born, Huntington, New York; student, St. Paul's School, Concord, New Hampshire, 1927-32; B.A., Yale University, 1936; M.A., Harvard University, 1939; instructor of government, Yale University, 1939-41; served with Office of Strategic Services, 1941-45; editor, Auburn (New York) *Citizen Advertiser*, 1946-48; chief editorial writer, New York *Herald Tribune*, 1948-56; director, The Twentieth Century Fund, 1956- ; special White House consultant on the arts, 1962; board member, Parsons School of Design; Art Commission of New York; chairman of board, Museum of Modern Art's International Council; trustee, Mt. Holyoke College; New School for Social Research; International House; St. Paul's School; president, Woodrow Wilson Foundation; fellow, Jonathan Edwards College, Yale University; decorated Chevalier in the French Legion of Honor, 1955; Phi Beta Kappa; author, *These Are the Days,* 1936; *The Woods Are Large; Remembrance of My Brother,* 1945; *A Pattern of Politics,* 1947; *The Politics of Woodrow Wilson; Selections from His Speeches and Writings,* 1956; co-author, *Diversity of Worlds; France and the United States Look at Their Common Problems,* 1957. (See also *Current Biography: 1958.*)

JACKSON, HENRY M. (1912-). Born, Everett, Washington; graduate of Everett high school, 1930; LL.B., University of Washington Law School, 1935; LL.D., University of Alaska; admitted to Washington state bar, 1935; prosecuting attorney, Snohomish county, 1938-40; United States House of Representatives (Democrat, Washington), 1941-52; army duty, 1943-44; chairman, committee on Indian Affairs, 1945-46; United States delegate, International Maritime Conference, 1946; United States Senate, 1953- ; member, Senate committees on Armed Services, Government Operations, and Interior and Insular Affairs. (See also *Current Biography: 1953.*)

KENNEDY, JOHN FITZGERALD (1917-). Born, Brookline, Massachusetts; student, London School of Economics, 1935-36; B.S., *cum laude,* Harvard University, 1940; LL.D., University of Notre Dame, 1950, Tufts College, 1954, Harvard University, 1956; served in United States Navy, 1941-45, awarded Purple Heart and other military decorations; correspondent, San Francisco United Nations Conference, British election, Potsdam Meeting, 1945; United States House of Representatives (Democrat, Massachusetts), 1947-53; United States Senate, 1953-60; elected President of the United States, 1960; author, *Why England Slept,* 1940; *Profiles in Courage,* 1956 (Pulitzer prize for biography); *The Strategy of Peace,* 1960. (See also *Current Biography: 1961.*)

LIPPMANN, WALTER (1889-). Born, New York City; A.B., Harvard University, 1910 (degree taken 1909); graduate work in philosophy; one-time associate editor, *The New Republic;* with New York *World,* 1921-31, as editor during latter part of period; joined New York *Herald Tribune* in 1931 as commentator on national and international affairs; assistant to Secretary of War, June-October 1917; member, Board of Overseers, Harvard University, 1933-39; Phi Beta Kappa; member, National Institute of Arts and Letters; member, American Academy of Arts and Letters; Pulitzer prize special citation, 1957; Pulitzer prize for reporting of international affairs, 1962; editor, *The Poems of Paul Mariett,* 1913; author of many works, including *Preface to Politics,* 1913; *The Stakes of Diplomacy,* 1915; *The Political Scene,* 1919; *Liberty and the News,* 1920; *Public Opinion,* 1922; *The Phantom Public,* 1925; *A Preface to Morals,* 1929; *Interpretations,* 1932; *Interpretations,* 1933-35; *The Method of Freedom,* 1934; *The Good Society,* 1937; *United States Foreign Policy: Shield of the Republic,* 1943; *The Public Philosophy,* 1955; *The Communist World and Ours,* 1959.

MINOW, NEWTON N. (1926-   ). Born, Milwaukee, Wisconsin; studied engineering at University of Michigan, Army Specialized Training Program; B.S., Northwestern University, 1949, with major in speech and political science; LL.B., Northwestern University School of Law; recipient of Wigmore Award; editor of *Illinois Law Review;* began association with Chicago law firms in 1950; with firm of which Adlai E. Stevenson was a member, 1955-61; law clerk to Chief Justice Fred M. Vinson, 1951; suggested presidential debates for Stevenson-Eisenhower in 1956; named one of the Ten Outstanding Young Men in Chicago, 1960; chairman, Federal Communications Commission, '1961-   ; received George Foster Peabody award for distinguished service to television and radio, 1961; contributor, *Journal of Criminal Law, Criminology, and Political Science.* (See also *Current Biography: 1961.*)

RUSK, DEAN (1909-   ). Born, Cherokee County, Georgia; A.B., Davidson College, 1931; B.S., St. John's College, Oxford University, 1933; M.A., 1934; LL.D., Mills College, 1948, Davidson College, 1950, University of California at Berkeley, 1961; associate professor of government and dean of the faculty, Mills College, 1934-40; assistant chief, Division of International Security Affairs, Department of State, 1946; special assistant to the Secretary of War, 1946-47; director, Office of United Nations Affairs, Department of State, 1948-49; first assistant Secretary of State for United Nations Affairs, February 1949; deputy Under Secretary of State, 1949-50; assistant Secretary of State for Far Eastern Affairs, 1950-51; president, Rockefeller Foundation, 1952-60; Secretary of State, 1961-   ; contributor to *America's Role in International Social Welfare,* 1955; contributor to *Foreign Affairs* and other periodicals. (See also *Current Biography: 1961.*)

SCANLAN, ROSS (1902-1961). Born, Albany, New York; A.B., Cornell University, 1925; A.M., University of Pittsburgh, 1927; Ph.D., Cornell University, 1937; early teaching of speech at University of Pittsburgh, Washington University, Cornell University, and Dartmouth College; advanced from tutor to full professor of speech, The City College of New York, 1934-61; exchange professor of speech, University of Hawaii, 1959-60; died, April 15, 1961; assistant editor, *Quarterly Journal of Speech,* 1951-53; associate editor, 1954-56, 1960-61; contributor to *Quarterly Journal of Speech* and *Speech Monographs;* co-author, *Speech Preparation and Delivery,* 1942; contributor to proceedings *Eastern Public Speaking Conference,* 1940; contributor to *Studies in Speech and Drama in Honor of Alexander M. Drummond,* 1944; contributor to *The Rhetorical Idiom,* 1958.

SEABORG, GLENN T. (1912-   ). Born, Ishpeming, Michigan; A.B., University of California at Los Angeles, 1934; Ph.D., University of California at Berkeley, 1937; instructor in chemistry, University of California at Berkeley, 1939-41; assistant professor, 1941; professor, 1945; announced discovery of plutonium (atomic number 94), 1940; associated with Manhattan Project on creation of atomic bomb; returned to teaching, 1946; associate director, Lawrence Radiation Laboratory, 1954-58; member of advisory committee to Atomic Energy Commission, 1946-50; shared Nobel prize in chemistry with E. M. McMillan for work on transuranium elements, 1951; Fermi Award, 1959; member of President Eisenhower's science advisory committee, 1959; chancellor, University of California at Berkeley, 1958-61; chairman, Atomic Energy Commission, 1961-   ; frequent contributor to scientific journals; co-author, *Comprehensive Inorganic Chemistry I,* 1953; *The Chemistry of the Actinide Elements,* 1957; *Elements of the Universe,* 1958. (See also *Current Biography: 1961.*)

SEARS, PAUL B. (1891-   ). Born, Bucyrus, Ohio; B.S., Ohio Wesleyan University, 1913; A.M., University of Nebraska, 1915; Ph.D., University of Chicago, 1922; honorary degrees from Ohio Wesleyan University, Marietta College, University of Nebraska, Wayne State University, Oberlin College, and University of Arkansas; instructor of botany, Ohio State University, 1915, 1919; assistant professor of botany, University of Nebraska, 1919-25; associate professor, 1925-27; professor of botany and head of department, University of Oklahoma, 1927-38; research associate, Teachers College, Columbia, 1936-38; professor of botany, Oberlin College, 1938-50; professor of conservation, Yale University, 1950-60; retired from active service, June 1960; Carnegie visiting professor of botany, University of Hawaii, September 1961-February 1962; Andersen visiting professor of American studies, Carleton College, 1962; president, Nebraska Academy of Science, 1924; general secretary, Botanical Society of America, 1924-28; president, American Association for the Advancement of Science, 1956; president, Ecological Society of America, 1948; president, American Society of Naturalists, 1959; board member, National Science Foundation; board member, National Audubon Society; author, *Deserts on the March*, 1935; *This Is Our World*, 1937; *Who Are These Americans?* 1939; *Life and Environment: The Interrelations of Living Things*, 1939; *This Useful World*, 1941; *Charles Darwin: The Naturalist as a Cultural Force*, 1950; *Where There Is Life*, 1962; author, various technical and other journal articles. (See also *Current Biography: 1960*.)

SMITH, MARGARET CHASE (1897-). Born, Skowhegan, Maine; graduate, Skowhegan high school, 1916; teacher in Skowhegan schools, 1916; executive officer, *Independent Reporter*, for eight years; treasurer, New England Waste Process Company, 1928; served on Republican State Committee of Maine, 1930-36; past president, Maine Federation of Business and Professional Women's Clubs; honorary degrees from many institutions, including Colby College, Temple University, Coe College, Columbia University, George Washington University, University of New Brunswick, University of North Carolina, and Bowdoin College; United States House of Representatives (Republican, Maine), 1940-48; United States Senate, 1949- ; member, Senate committees on Armed Services, Appropriations, and Aeronautical and Space Sciences. (See also *Current Biography: March 1962*.)

STANTON, FRANK (1908-). Born, Muskegon, Michigan; A.B., Ohio Wesleyan University, 1930; A.M., Ohio State University, 1932; Ph.D., 1935; LL.D., Ohio Wesleyan University, 1946; LL.D., Birmingham-Southern College, 1946; instructor in psychology, Ohio State University, 1932-35; joined Columbia Broadcasting System, 1935; research staff, 1935-38; director of research, 1938-42; vice president and general executive, 1942-46; vice president and general manager, 1945-46; president, 1946- ; associate director, Office of Radio Research, Princeton University, 1937-40; member of advisory council of Office of Radio Research, Columbia University, 1940; trustee, Rand Corporation; director, New York Life Insurance Company; fellow, American Psychological Association; member of many councils, associations, and societies; recipient, 1962 gold medal of the Radio and Television

Executives Society; co-author, *Students' Guide—The Study of Psychology*, 1935; film editor, *Some Psychological Reactions to Emotional Stimuli*, 1932; *Factors in Visual Depth Perception*, 1939; co-editor, *Radio Research*, 1941, 1942-43.

TOYNBEE, ARNOLD JOSEPH (1889-). Born, London, England; student, Winchester College, 1902-07; Balliol College, Oxford University, 1907-11; British Archaeological School, Athens, 1911-12; Litt.D., Oxford University, Cambridge University, Birmingham University; D.C.L., Princeton University; LL.D., Columbia University; fellow and tutor, Balliol College, Oxford University, 1912-15; in government service, 1915-19; professor of Byzantine and modern Greek language, literature and history, University of London, 1919-24; emeritus professor since 1924; director, Foreign Research and Press Service, Royal Institute of International Affairs, 1939-43; director, research department, Foreign Office, 1943-46; member, British delegation to Peace Conference in Paris, 1946; director of studies, Royal Institute of International Affairs, 1925-55; decorated Companion of Honor, 1956; fellow, British Academy; author of many books, including *Nationality and War*, 1915; *Greek Historical Thought*, 1924; *The World after the Peace Conference*, 1925; *A Journey to China*, 1931; *A Study of History*, 1934-54, *Civilization on Trial*, 1948; *War and Civilization*, 1951; *An Historian's Approach to Religion*, 1956; *East to West: A Journey Round the World*, 1958; *Reconsiderations*, 1961. (See also *Current Biography: 1947*.)

WRISTON, HENRY M. (1889-). Born, Laramie, Wyoming; A.B., Wesleyan University (Connecticut), 1911; A.M., 1912; Ph.D., Harvard University, 1922; many honorary degrees, including LL.D., Ripon College, 1926, Wesleyan University, 1931, Rutgers University, 1940, Princeton University, 1946, Harvard University, 1949; Litt.D., Columbia University, 1937; L.H.D., Wesleyan University, 1943; active in debating at Wesleyan University; instructor, associate professor, professor of history, Wesleyan University, 1914-25; chief secretary, Round Tables of Institute of Politics, Williamstown, Massachusetts, 1922-26; president, Lawrence College, 1925-37; president, Brown University, 1937-55; now president emeritus; president, American Assembly, 1958- ; chairman, President's Commission on National

Goals; author of many works including *War Chest Practice*, 1918; *Nature of a Liberal College*, 1937; *Prepare for Peace*, 1941; *Challenge to Freedom*, 1943; *Strategy of Peace*, 1944; *Diplomacy in a Democracy*, 1956; *Wriston Speaking*, 1957; *Academic Procession*, 1959. (See also *Current Biography: 1952*.)

CUMULATIVE AUTHOR INDEX
1960-1961—1961-1962

A cumulative author index to the volumes of REPRESENTATIVE AMERICAN SPEECHES for the years 1937-1938 through 1959-1960 appears in the 1959-1960 volume.